SETH MacFARLANE'S

A MILLION WAYS TO DIE IN THE WEST

A NOVEL

Written by
SETH MacFARLANE

Based on a screenplay written by
**SETH MacFARLANE & ALEC SULKIN
& WELLESLEY WILD**

CANONGATE
Edinburgh · London

This edition published by Canongate Books in 2014

First published in Great Britain in 2014 by Canongate Books Ltd,
14 High Street, Edinburgh EH1 1TE

www.canongate.tv

2

This novel is based on a screenplay by Seth MacFarlane,
Alec Sulkin and Wellesley Wild.

First published in the United States by Ballantine Books,
an imprint of Random House, a division of Random House LLC,
a Penguin Random House Company, New York.

British Library Cataloguing-in-Publication Data

A catalogue record for this book is available on
request from the British Library

ISBN 978 1 78211 358 4

Text design by Christopher Zucker
Printed and bound in Great Britain by Clays Ltd, St Ives plc

A
MILLION
WAYS TO DIE IN THE WEST

Albert Stark was a coward. Not a quivering, jittery, weak-kneed sort of a coward, but the kind who viewed his cowardice as an act of sensibility: a coward in the name of pragmatism. To Albert, his cowardice functioned as a shield that existed to service the very sensible goal of self-preservation. In the West, brave men got killed. Cowards stayed alive.

Death was everywhere on the frontier.

"Everything that's not you wants you dead," Albert would often say. "Outlaws, Indians, angry gamblers, disgruntled prostitutes, wild animals, the weather, disease—hell, even a trip to the dentist means taking your fucking life in your hands."

One needed only to glance at the front page of any local newspaper to see the truth in such a point of view:

INFANT TRAMPLED BY SICKLY MARE

HUNDREDS PERISH IN LATE SPRING DAMP

SCHOOLMARM FELLED BY TUMBLEWEED ABRASION

MASS HANGING GOES WELL

MUD DEATHS REACH 30-YEAR HIGH

DUTCH FAMILY CRUSHED BY FALLING CHINAMEN

WOMAN FOUND GUILTY OF ADULTERY; TONGUE, BREASTS REMOVED

50-ACRE BUFFALO HERD DESTROYS TOWN

WATER TOWER CONTAMINATED BY BATHING NEGRESS

BLACK BEARS FEAST ON KINDERGARTEN CLASS

HAIL STORM DRIVES SNAKES INTO LOCAL CHURCH—NO SURVIVORS

Yes, it seemed to Albert that fear was a very useful thing for a man living in the southern Arizona territory.

So on this blistering hot day he was quite content to once again allow cowardice to insulate him from an early demise.

He stood at the center of the thoroughfare, gun belt at the ready—or so it appeared. The townsfolk of Old Stump lined the street, eager as ever to witness that most electrifying of all frontier spectacles:

the showdown. But at the moment, Albert stood alone. His opponent was nowhere to be seen, and high noon had officially come and gone. No one spoke, save for the occasional fluttering murmurs of slightly confused anticipation from the onlookers. Dirt farmers watched patiently. Women fanned themselves, desperately attempting to force a few little bursts of air between their numerous layers of clothing. Well-to-do gentlemen checked their pocket watches and smoked the sort of fine cigars one can only truly enjoy outdoors in 112-degree weather. Children fidgeted and played idly with their favorite toys, such as apple cores, bits of string, and deceased mice. Dogs lay panting on the ground, no doubt wondering how the fuck any human being could live a non-suicidal existence in such an awful, depressing place.

Albert tried to avoid eye contact with the surrounding spectators, aside from the occasional shared glance with a strikingly beautiful blond-haired woman who stood on the steps in front of the general store. She offered him a wan smile, perhaps meant to be reassuring but with a seemingly dubious degree of conviction.

And then, at last, they heard the sound of approaching hoofbeats. Very faint and distant at first, then more distinct, until finally a man rode into view at the opposite end of the thoroughfare. He slowed his horse with a sharp yank on the reins that appeared to startle the animal, though it came to an obedient halt. The man dismounted and moved with a decided lack of urgency into position at the end of the street.

Albert stiffened and regarded his opponent. Charlie Blanche and Albert Stark could not have been more contrasting in their deportment: Blanche was a grizzled, weathered-looking mass of aggression, who looked as though he hadn't smiled since the days of Lewis and Clark. He glared at Albert with an expression that seemed to say, *I want to shoot you in the dick with a bullet made of cancer.*

Albert cleared his throat. "So . . . I guess high noon to you means 12:15?"

Charlie stared blankly for a beat. "What?"

"Well," said Albert, genuinely annoyed in spite of his fear, "I mean, you said high noon, and I was here, and . . . I've sort of just been waiting."

Blanche narrowed his eyes darkly. "I'm here now."

"Yeah, I know, but it's just—it's like sort of inconsiderate, because it's like you're saying that your time is more valuable than everyone else's, and . . . well, I know everybody here has like a full day, and they all took time off to be here, and—I mean, right, everyone?"

No one answered. Albert looked around furtively

in search of a supportive face but found none. His gaze landed on a toothless old man who did not look like he had a full day at all. The man stared emptily, his tongue sliding along the perimeter of his solitary tooth, like a sentry dutifully patrolling the last remaining outpost of an all-but-defeated army.

"Draw," said Charlie Blanche.

A wave of renewed alertness swept over the onlookers as they shared a collective inhalation. Now the show would begin!

Albert took a deep breath of his own. "Um . . . no."

A perplexed buzzing from the townsfolk. The pretty blond woman regarded Albert with a look of confused dismay.

"What do you mean, no?" Blanche narrowed his eyes further, nearly squinting them out of existence.

Albert took another deep breath. "I . . . I don't wanna do this. You're a way better shot than me, and so before this gets outta hand and we both get all crazy and dead here, I . . . I don't wanna have a shoot-out."

"You yellow, Stark?" The corner of Blanche's mouth twisted into a perversion of a half smile—no doubt the warmest expression his long-rotted disposition would accommodate.

"Well, look, *yellow* is kind of a"—Albert paused uneasily—"I mean, that's kind of racist to our hard-working friends from the Far East, right, guys?"

He turned to a small cluster of Chinese railroad workers watching from off to the side. Surely now he'd get a small boost of support. The shortest Chinaman gave him the finger.

"O-okay," Albert stuttered. "Welcome."

Blanche barked out a gravelly laugh. "Even the damn *Chinese* know you're yellow!"

Albert turned back to face his adversary. "Look, I—I just wanna resolve things more reasonably, okay? I mean, we're both intelligent adults, right? So . . . I'm just gonna pay you for the damages."

Blanche's expression did not change. "Suits me fine. That's fifty dollars."

"Right, okay," said Albert, fidgeting slightly. "Now, here's the thing . . . I don't have fifty dollars in cash—"

Charlie's hand moved toward the butt of his gun.

"—*but* . . . I will give you twenty-five sheep."

Charlie's index finger was almost touching the trigger. "I don't want sheep, Stark."

Heat sweat was suddenly interfused with panic sweat as Albert realized he was in trouble. "Well, this—this is a lotta sheep. This is like twenty-five sheep. Like a whole . . . gaggle. A pack? Is it a pack?" He laughed anxiously as his floundering brain let loose a diarrhetic stream of nonsense. "Oh, my God, can you believe this?! I'm a sheep farmer, and I'm totally blanking on the plural—is it a *school* of sheep? I don't know! Ha! Hey, you know what a group of ferrets is called? A *business*. A business of ferrets. English is fun, 'cause there's all kinds of secret treasures—"

The *crack* of a bullet split the air as Charlie Blanche fired a shot at Albert's feet. Albert jumped back with a distinctly feminine shriek.

"Your goddamn sheep grazed up half my ranch, Stark! That grass ain't never gonna grow back."

There was a deep-rooted hatred for sheepmen among the cattle ranchers of the West, largely because the sheep themselves grazed in such a deep-rooted fashion. They would devour the grass so close to the ground that, if left unchecked, they could effectively strip a pasture bare to the point that the grass had to be resown. *No cow can graze where a sheep has been,* the cattlemen would declare. As a result, range wars often broke out between cattle and sheep farmers, with terribly bloody consequences. It also didn't help that sheepmen were generally considered huge pussies.

Albert swallowed what little saliva he had left as Charlie raised his gun and took aim.

"Okay, okay!" Albert threw up his hands in a gesture of surrender. "I'll sell off the sheep myself, all right? I'll get you the money! O-okay? You'll have it tomorrow."

There was a terrifying moment during which Albert was certain that, even though he had truckled to his opponent's demands, Blanche would pull the trigger. But, instead, the other man slowly lowered the pistol. "If I don't have that cash, I'm comin' after you. And I'll shoot you three times: forehead, nose, and chin, so your head splits clean in half like a fairground watermelon."

"Oh, and I would deserve it," Albert blurted obsequiously. "In that scenario? Oh, my God, what a jerk I would be. But I—that's not the kind of guy I am, so I—I'll get you your money."

Charlie Blanche carefully holstered his weapon. Albert let loose a quivering exhale as Blanche moved back toward his horse. *I'm so glad I didn't pee,* thought Albert, feeling an aftershock of panic over how truly close he'd come to death. He turned and walked back up the street, his legs feeling like they were made of jam—

CRACK!!

The townsfolk gasped. Albert collapsed to the ground as an unimaginably cutting pain blasted through his ankle. "FUCK!" he screamed as he turned in shock.

Charlie had shot him.

"Just a little taste," said Blanche in a soft, deadly

tone. He reholstered his pistol, mounted his horse, and loped off without another word.

And almost immediately the townsfolk began to disperse as if nothing had happened. The entertainment was over. Everyone casually returned to their day as if they'd just finished watching a sideshow in a traveling carnival—never mind the fact that a man had barely avoided losing his life mere moments before.

A pudgy, slightly balding man in his mid-thirties hurried to where Albert lay clutching his foot in pain.

"Aw, man, Albert! You okay?"

Albert had never been shot before, but he'd witnessed men who had. And those little metal pellets could do some horrifically gruesome damage. He sucked in a sharp breath of air as he steeled himself and pulled back his trouser leg. Though the pain was intolerable, a look of surprise came over his face as he registered the superficiality of the wound. It had pierced the skin, but not by much. *Jesus, how the hell bad must the pain be from a dead-on shot?*

"It's—it's fine, it's just grazed," Albert said, pulling his trouser leg back down.

"Oh, thank God." Edward breathed a sigh of relief.

Edward Phelps was a kind-eyed, mild-mannered

cobbler and Albert's closest friend. Out on the frontier, however, that didn't necessarily mean an inseparable bond. In a town of fewer than seventy-five people, your choices were limited when it came to picking a best pal. Albert liked Edward well enough, but it had more to do with the fact that Edward was one of the few people in the West who wouldn't shoot you for looking at him the wrong way. Albert wasn't sure, but he didn't think Edward even owned a gun. And if he did, it would have looked completely out of place. If there were such a term as *aggressively affable,* that was Edward.

A much more imposing man approached the center of the thoroughfare.

"You all right, Stark?" Sheriff Arness inquired without expression.

"Yeah, I'm fine," Albert responded. "Oh, hey, listen, Sheriff, I wanna thank you for your help. Appreciate you stepping in and halting this deadly altercation going on right in front of your office. Really terrific, thanks for the support."

The sheriff looked at Albert with coldness. "It's not my place to intervene, Stark. I believe a man should fight his own battles."

Albert stared for a beat. This guy was everything that was fucked up about the frontier, all wrapped up in one tough-eyed, sunburned package sealed with a tin star. "You're the sheriff," Albert said, trying not to sound too much like he was talking to a five-year-old.

"That's right."

"So . . . the one thing we're all paying you to do—like, the one function you have in town—you're saying everyone else should do it."

"I'm not your goddamn bodyguard, Stark."

Once again, Albert resisted the urge to sound as if he were teaching a class of retarded children. "Well, actually, yes. See, as the sheriff, it's technically kind of your job to protect my body from harm."

"Yeah, it is kinda your job," Edward chimed in, always the faithful, supportive pal who didn't know when to keep his mouth closed.

"Shut up," the sheriff snapped, and Edward quickly lowered his head and shuffled aside timidly. The sheriff turned back to Albert. "I guess you and I see things differently."

"So, like, if you opened a restaurant, would you wait for people to come in and then say, 'A man should cook his own food'?"

"You'd best watch your tongue, or you're gonna find yourself in a jail cell."

"Oh, *there* we go!" Albert threw up his arms, the stress and pain of the day exploding in an outburst of aggravation. "The long arm of the law finally lashes out to protect *itself* against pissy people!"

The sheriff just glared. "You should see Doctor Harper about that ankle," he said at last, turning away stiffly.

Albert expelled a pained sigh of defeat, struggled to pull himself up from the dirt, and limped off toward the doctor's office.

Frontier medicine was essentially an oxymoron.

The big city hospitals in 1882 were bad enough, but they exemplified the cutting edge of science compared to what sort of treatment you got out West.

The medical office of Doctor Matthew Harper, the only licensed practicing physician in the town of Old Stump, was a glorified shack. His hand-painted shingle swayed and creaked in the hot, dusty wind—a fine indication of the kind of care you could expect if you fell ill in this little community. Inside, the wooden shelves were lined with various bottles of medicines, elixirs, tonics—but who the hell was anybody kidding? It was all just liquor. On the frontier, medicine was merely booze with a fancy label.

Doctor Harper stood over the body of his patient. She was a woman in her forties, hard-lined and graying. She lay unconscious from the doctor's ether, which was a good thing, since her abdomen was sliced wide open. Doctor Harper's hands were covered in blood as he meticulously worked away at her insides, using all the skills his dental training had provided him. A mangy-looking housecat leapt up onto the operating table, sniffing at the body.

"Oh, come on, now, you know you're not supposed to be up here," Doctor Harper chuckled, scooping up the cat and placing him gently on the floor. "You run along now, Jesus, you hear?" The doctor's hands left smears of blood on the cat's fur, at which it eagerly lapped. Harper returned to his work, brushing the errant feline hairs off the table.

"Hello?" came a voice from the outer room. "Doctor Harper?"

Harper wiped his hands on a rag, tossed it on his patient's leg, and strolled into the outer room. Albert had already seated himself in a chair, eager to take the weight off his injured limb.

"Hi, Doc," he said. "I was wondering if—*holy shit*." He stopped mid-sentence as he registered Doctor Harper's hands, which were still shiny with fresh crimson blood.

"Oh, don't mind this," Doctor Harper reassured him. "I'm just in the middle of surgery."

"I can come back," Albert said, moving toward the door.

"No, no, she'll be out for a while. It's Mrs. Callaghan, poor woman. Her stomach devil was about to explode, so I had to take it out."

It took Albert a beat to decipher that one. "Her appendix?"

"Yep, that's the fella," the doctor answered.

Albert wondered why he had even come here. A trip to the doctor's office was likely to turn a hangnail into a desperate struggle for survival.

"Now, what's the trouble?" Doctor Harper asked, allowing himself a swallow from one of the bottles on the shelf. No doubt such frequent behavior contributed to the heavily seamed face and unhealthy pallor that brought to mind Luke 4:23: *Physician, heal thyself.*

"Uh, it's a bullet graze. Just need it checked out."

"Oh, yeah." The doctor smiled with a gossip-hungry glint in his eye. "I heard you turned yellow on Charlie Blanche."

"Well, Doc, I know you'd rather be patching up a gaping chest wound than a minor graze, but unfortunately I value my life. Now, you wanna take a look at this, or should I limp out into the desert and let the fucking coyotes have at it?"

"All right, let's have a look." Doctor Harper laughed good-naturedly. The doctor rolled up Albert's trouser leg, his hands leaving light bloody smears on the fabric, courtesy of Mrs. Callaghan.

"I notice you're not big on the hand-washing," Albert remarked listlessly. The doctor either ignored the comment or was too busy focusing on the injury.

"Ooh, that's a nasty one," he observed, examining the wound. "We may have to take that off, otherwise you could wind up with a case of toe-foot."

Albert sighed. "Okay, first of all, I don't think that's a real thing, and second of all, it's a graze, Doc. I'm not gonna let you cut my foot off."

"Suit yourself. But I've seen toe-foot turn into knee-leg in less than a week."

"Just a dressing, thanks," Albert responded curtly, now even more anxious to get this over with as quickly as possible.

Doctor Harper pulled open a drawer and retrieved a roll of bandages as Albert surveyed the small office. The remains of a roast chicken were scattered on a plate next to an open jar of laudanum, and a recently lit cigar sat precariously on the edge of a side table, its pointy tip still darkened with saliva. As for any sign of official physician's credentials, the sole candidate hung in a wooden frame on the far wall.

"*Texas Territory Medical College*," Albert read the handwritten diploma aloud as the doctor went to work on his leg. "So, is that a pretty prestigious place?"

"Yessir, third in my class," Harper answered with genuine pride.

"Ah. And was this an indoor medical school?" Albert asked without a trace of sarcasm or irony.

"All right, there we go," said the doctor, straightening up and smiling down at the new dressing. "Try to stay off it for a bit."

Albert looked at the results. "Just a dry cloth bandage? That's it?"

"Well, what else would you like me to do?"

"Clean it, maybe?" Albert answered, feigning patience. "So I don't get an infection and die?"

"Well, now, that's up to the Lord God."

Albert stared for a beat. "I guess I'm looking for someone more reliable."

They wished each other good day as Jesus the cat helped himself to Mrs. Callaghan's large intestine.

On any given evening, the Old Stump Saloon was packed to the gills with gamblers, boozers, and unshaven purveyors of various foul smells. At times, in fact, there seemed to be virtually hundreds of different odors, all fiercely competing for dominance in the confined and poorly ventilated space.

But at two o'clock in the afternoon, the place was mostly deserted. A couple of frail-looking old cowhands sat at the bar staring into their glasses, but otherwise the lower level was empty.

Except for Edward Phelps.

Edward sat patiently on a wooden chair at the base of the stairwell that led up to the brothel rooms. He probably should have brought a book or something, he thought, but the wait wouldn't be too long. In his hand he held a lovely late-spring bouquet of daisies, lilacs, and daffodils. From upstairs, the raucous sounds of sexual intercourse could be heard as Edward's girlfriend, Ruth, was fucked wildly by a dirty cowboy.

"Oh, yes! *YES!!*" she screamed, her voice reverberating throughout the saloon.

"Yeah, you like me fuckin' you, don't you?" bellowed the dirty cowboy.

"Yes! Yes, it's really terrific!" she shouted back between moans of ecstasy.

"I got dirt on my dick from workin' outside all day!"

"I know! I love the scratchy feeling inside me!"

"Yeah, you *like* the dirt on my dick, don't you?!"

"I do! I really do! It's such a treat!"

Ruth's sex talk had always been a bit clumsy, but her heart was in the right place, and as a prostitute she was exemplary: always on time for her shift, freshly bathed after every fifth customer, and willing to accommodate all types of fetishes. Edward admired her work ethic. The seriousness with which a person took professional obligations said a lot about their character. He was lucky to be with such a woman.

"Stick your finger in my asshole!" shouted the dirty cowboy.

"I'm excited to!" Ruth answered.

At that moment, Millie, the house madam, descended the stairs. She was plump, in her early forties, with the saucy, painted look of a career saloon whore. Her thick mound of done-up hair, no doubt once dark as onyx, now showed numerous streaks of gray. As she approached, she waved a beringed hand in the cobbler's direction.

"Hi, Edward," she said with a smile. Her cherry-red lips and heavily rouged cheeks, while undignified-looking in and of themselves, at least added some welcome color to the brown-on-brown room.

"Oh, hey, Millie." Edward grinned, standing respectfully.

"You waiting for Ruth?"

"Yeah, I got off work a little early, so I thought I'd take her out for a picnic."

"Oh. You're a good boyfriend."

"I try to be."

Millie glanced toward the upper level. "Well, it sounds like she's almost done," she said, as the moans of orgasmic passion reached a dissonant crescendo.

"*OH, GOD, I'M GONNA COME!*" Ruth screamed.

"Those are pretty flowers," Millie remarked.

Edward looked down at his bouquet with a proud grin. "I know, aren't they beautiful? There are even a couple of tulips in here. They're hard to come by this time of year, but Ruth is very particular."

"*OH, YES! SHOOT THAT DIRTY COWBOY CUM ALL OVER MY FACE!*"

Edward adjusted his tie, hearing that Ruth was almost finished. "Do I look all right?" he asked, presenting himself to Millie for inspection.

"Yes, you're . . . you're fine," she answered, unable to contain her curiosity any longer. "Say, Edward . . . can I ask you something?"

"Sure."

"Are you . . . okay with the fact that your girlfriend gets screwed by about fifteen guys every day and gets paid to do it?"

"Oh. Well, I mean, my job sucks too."

"Yeah, but you repair shoes."

"Ugh, don't remind me!" Edward laughed. "The shoe business has been so slow since the Civil War ended."

"Really?"

"Yeah, there's just a lot less legs."

Millie was about to press the original issue a bit

further, when Ruth came bounding down the stairs, still in the process of pulling her clothes back on.

"Eddie, is that you?" she squealed happily.

He whirled around to meet her eyes and flung his arms wide open. "Hey, sweetheart!"

"What are you doing here?" she exclaimed, smothering him in a joyous embrace and kissing him flush on the lips.

He flinched. "Ooh, your breath is a little . . ."

"Sorry—I had to give a blow job." She covered her mouth, her already red cheeks coloring just a bit more.

Edward smiled with genuine understanding. "That's okay. Hey, I got done a little early, and I thought we could go for a walk out by the stream."

Ruth hugged him all over again for his thoughtfulness. "Ohhh, you are the *best*! Yeah, c'mon, let's go!" She gave him a peck on the cheek, then looked at Millie. "Don't I have the best boyfriend in the world?"

Millie opened her mouth to respond, but nothing seemed fitting.

"Bye!" Ruth giggled, pulling a beaming Edward by the hand toward the saloon doors. "What time should I be back?" she asked, turning briefly back to Millie.

"Well, Clyde Hodgkins wanted to know if he could come by later on."

"Oh—what's he want?" Ruth asked.

"I think he wants anal."

Ruth whirled around and grabbed Edward's hands. "Oh, honey! We could afford to get you a new belt for church!"

Edward's eyes widened as he registered his good fortune. "Wow, that'd be great!"

"I know!" Ruth erupted with delight, squeezing his hands and swinging them back and forth in a dancerly fashion.

"So, what time will you need her? 5:30 or so?" Edward asked Millie.

"Well, this isn't really like a dentist's office, Edward. He'll probably stop in when he's ready to put his penis inside an asshole."

"Okay, we'll say 5:00 just to be safe," Edward said. And, with that, the couple hurried out into the afternoon sunlight, their love for each other outshining the brightness of the day.

Deadcow Bridge had earned its name back around the time that Old Stump's first settlers rode west with dreams of making a new life for themselves. In addition to its human complement, the wagon train had brought with it two hundred head of beef cattle. But when the settlers reached the southwestern Arizona territory, the herd had succumbed to a mysterious illness and was decimated within a matter of days. In light of their misfortune, the weary pioneers decided to halt their westward journey and build their community on the spot. The terrain was somewhat rocky and not particularly forgiving, but the discovery of a nearby river revealed more desirable land beyond. However, when the company tried to cross the river, they found it to be too deep. A lack of passable shallows for some distance in either direction left the group stymied and frustrated. Then one of the wives came up with a novel solution: The settlers dragged all the cow corpses down to the river, and piled them up in the water. After a time, the pile became high enough that the settlers could use it as a bridge of sorts, allowing them to cross the river to the land beyond, which would eventually become Old Stump. Of course, the massive amount of decomposing bovine flesh in the water caused an epidemic that quickly wiped out the entire population. But the next settlers who arrived built a wooden bridge and crossed the river with ease, where they founded the town of Old Stump. Deadcow Bridge was hence named in tribute to the memory of the first settlers, and their tragic deaths from dead cow water.

It was there in the cool shade of the bridge that Albert sat sharing a picnic of fried chicken and fresh-baked bread with his girlfriend, Louise. The two had been together for a year and a half, and Albert counted himself extremely fortunate to have her in his life. She was a rare beauty, even discounting the standards of the western frontier, where most women were indistinguishable from bears. She had all her teeth too, which was another wondrous anomaly. Albert would often sit on the front porch with his arm around Louise, counting her teeth as they watched the setting of the desert sun.

Louise sat on the picnic blanket, her blond locks fluttering in the soft breeze, mimicking the gentle purling of the river waters. Her pale skin glowed with youth as she nibbled absently at a piece of bread with jam. She listened to Albert venting his frustration over the outcome of the day as she gazed out at the thousand tiny slices of white light flickering atop the lazy river.

"—I mean, that should've been the end of it, right?" he groused. "I tell him I'll pay him off, we go our separate ways, and that's it. But, no, the guy shoots me in the foot! Fuckin' douche."

He had been ranting for several minutes before he noticed that Louise appeared to be deliberately avoiding eye contact.

"What's the matter?" he asked.

Louise looked down at her hands for a beat, then said the last thing Albert expected to hear. "You should've fought him, Albert."

Albert stared at her with all the comprehension of a horse being asked to roll a cigarette. "Wait, *what*?"

"You should've fought Charlie Blanche." All of a sudden, she had no difficulty meeting his gaze.

"Wha—are you putting me on?"

"We don't know if your sheep grazed on his ranch," she said. "It could've been Hurley's cows. He should have to prove it, and he can't. So, I dunno . . . You should've fought him."

"Oh, my God, you're serious."

She nodded.

"Louise," he sputtered, "the guy's one of the best shots in the whole town! I mean, I look like I have Parkinson's next to him."

"What's Parkinson's?"

"Oh, just another way God mysteriously shows that he loves us. Look, I tried to psych myself up for the gunfight, but at the end of the day I'd rather not commit fucking suicide."

And then, from out of nowhere, lightning struck. "Albert . . . I'm breaking up with you."

When a parent, a sibling, or a close friend dies suddenly, the mind has an uncanny ability to process the news as a mistake, or fiction, or at worst a temporary reality that will surely correct itself in short order. The same sort of self-defense mechanism was activating within Albert's mind right now.

"Wh . . . what?"

"I'm sorry." She gave him a loving look, but it was all wrong. It took him a moment to realize it wasn't love he was seeing but rather sympathy. The look was one you might give a hospital patient before you told him the doctors were unable to save his balls.

Albert opened his mouth to speak, and what came out was, "I got shot today."

"I know," she answered.

Clearly she didn't hear what I said, he thought. *"Ow,"* he uttered, hoping that would drive the point home.

"I'm sorry you're hurt," she said, though to Albert she didn't sound sorry enough.

His mental gears were now restarting their grind, and he began to process exactly what was happening. He was being dumped. "Louise, I—*why?* Because of a *gunfight?*"

"No, it's not that. I mean, I guess maybe it gave me the little push I needed to finally come out and tell you—"

"Finally? What do you mean, finally? How long have you been planning this?!"

"God, you make it sound so malicious. I didn't plan this, Albert. But . . . I *have* been feeling this way for a while. It's . . . Look, you're a really great guy. I've just . . . I've realized I want something else."

The punches just kept on coming. Albert felt like

he might throw up, and he hoped the words would beat the vomit to his mouth. "Louise, I love you! What else could you want? You're my whole life! I've done everything for you for the past year and a half! Look, I know I'm only a sheep farmer, but I'm saving money, and as soon as—"

"Yeah, but you're not even a good sheep farmer, Albert," she interrupted. The sympathy in her expression was gone, and it seemed she was now beginning to offer her uncensored point of view. "I mean, your sheep are *everywhere*. The *one thing* a sheep farmer has to do is keep all his sheep in one place. I stopped by your farm the other day, and there was a sheep in the backyard, three way up on the ridge, two in the pond, and one on the roof."

"That's Bridget—she has a problem with retardation, but she's full of love. Look, I think we're getting off-track here," Albert said, desperation taking over his tone. "Louise, if it's not about the gunfight, tell me what it is! Tell me what the problem is, and maybe we can fix it!"

"Albert, you're a good guy, for sure," she responded, her voice softening once again to counter the sting of what she was about to say. "You're . . . not good for *me*. I don't wanna date *anybody* right now. I kinda have to deal with my own shit."

"Shit? What shit? We live in a frontier town in the middle of the goddamn desert! There isn't enough shit around for you to have any shit to deal with! My God, Louise, it's been a year and a half! We talked about getting married!"

"Listen, if I was older, maybe the timing would be right, but I don't wanna settle down yet. People are living to be 35 these days, so a girl doesn't have to get married right away. I sorta have to work on myself right now."

That was too much for Albert. *"I have to work on myself?"* he exclaimed. "Louise, that's what girls say when they have a good thing staring them in the face and they're too up their own ass to know what to do with it. I *know* you. You're not up your own ass. You're out here. Outside your ass. Where I can see you. And . . . you're the most beautiful woman I've ever known."

She spread her soft, white hands in a gesture that indicated quite clearly that she had nothing more to offer on the subject. "I don't know what else to tell you, Albert. It's over. I don't want to be with you anymore."

His mind was locking up again. "Wow," he said quietly, the hurt coating his voice with a quavering thickness. "Louise . . . I love you."

"I'm sorry."

Then, with nothing more than a defeated shrug, she stood up and walked away.

And as Albert Stark sat among the long shadows

that striped the golden glaze of the dying afternoon, he knew his life was over.

The sunset streaked across the Arizona sky, its miles and miles of titanic painted strokes illuminating the distant mesas, turning them a velvety pink. To an observer visiting the territory for the first time, the nightly visual feast would have been a breathtaking sight to behold. And though the spectacle was a regular one for him, viewed every evening from the front porch of his little farmhouse, Albert himself was not immune to its eye-popping chromatic sumptuousness. Tonight, however, he took no notice.

He rode toward his farm, stricken by a deadness of limb that twice nearly caused him to fall off his horse. Luckily for Albert, however, Curtis had been with him for almost eight years, and never was there a more reliable animal. Any horse will adapt to the rhythms of its rider, but equestrian skill had deftly avoided Albert; he was unbalanced and uncoordinated. His friends had all assumed that enough years in the saddle would solve the problem, but he simply had never improved.

But Curtis had. The horse would instinctively adjust his own weight to accommodate Albert's lapses, an astonishing mark of intuitive protectiveness that made Albert love him more than he loved any human being.

Except, of course, Louise.

Her face hovered before him all the way home, the ghost of a severed appendage. In the image, she burst forth with an amaranthine smile that spoke lovingly of every shared experience now rendered hollow. *That Louise still exists somewhere,* he told himself. *I just have to find her.* Only when he neared the farm did he begin to emerge from the delusional haze. The bleating of his sheep jerked him back to reality with a sharp stab of sound.

Albert grappled for control of his catatonic stare, and surveyed his withering corral. The wooden fences were crumbling and badly in need of repair. And, as usual, there were sheep all over the place. Some were inside the corral, others were out in the yard, and, sure enough, there was Bridget, looking lost and confused up on the roof. For the life of him, Albert could not figure out how the fuck she kept getting up there. In his mind, he could hear Louise's admonishing voice. She may have been wrong to dump him, but she was right about one thing: He was a shitty sheepman.

Albert shuffled into the farmhouse and hung his hat on the wooden peg next to the door. His mother and father, Elsie and George, glanced up from their wooden chairs on the other side of the room. For as long as Albert could remember, they had sat in those chairs all evening, every evening, Elsie sewing and George reading the Bible. And with both of them in their early seventies, that didn't seem likely to change.

"You're late," his father grunted.

"For what?" Albert asked.

There was a pause. "Fair enough," his father answered, and returned to his scripture.

That would be the extent of the evening's conversation. All in all, a lively, textured discussion compared to most nights.

Albert retreated into his dark little room and knelt down to reach under the bed. He pulled out a small, unmarked wooden box and carried it out to the front porch. The sun was sinking fast below the horizon. Albert lit a kerosene lamp and placed it next to the rickety old rocking chair that probably had only another six months left before it collapsed beneath some unlucky behind. He sat down and opened the box.

Inside were sepia-toned memories: the grand history of the great lovers Albert Stark and Louise Daniels. In actuality, there were only three pictures, but since photographs were hard to come by, Albert considered it a treasure trove. As he stared longingly at the shadows of better days frozen in time, he heard the approaching *clip-clop* of hoofbeats. He looked up and saw Edward and Ruth approaching in their tottery little buggy. *A happy couple,* he thought, with a twinge of resentment, then quickly and silently chided himself for the unwarranted burst of negativity. These were his friends, and they wanted to help. Nonetheless, his reaction was only human: To the man in a secure relationship, love was a bountiful feast to be enjoyed by all in attendance. But to the man without a companion, the feast was watched bitterly from outside through a frosted window, with the growl of a starving belly gurgling up from below.

Albert offered them a bloodless smile. "Hey, guys."

"Albert, we just heard about Louise," Edward said, climbing down from the buggy. "That's horrible! How are you holding up?"

"We're so sorry," Ruth added, dismounting after him with what seemed to be a wince of pain. "Are you doing okay?"

"Not really, no," Albert sighed, not having the energy to lie for their comfort. "You guys wanna sit down?"

"Yes, thanks," Edward said, and pulled up a wooden stool.

"I'm okay standing," said Ruth. "I had a long day at work."

Albert turned his attention back to the pictures in

his lap. "I was just looking at some old photographs of Louise and me." He held them up for his friends to see. They gazed dutifully at the images, even though they had seen them many times. "This was from the carnival. . . . Here we are at the town picnic . . . Oh, and this was the square dance." His face was an inexpressive mask, much like the faces in the pictures. "Y'know, I almost wish you could smile in photographs. Louise has such an incredible smile."

"That'd be weird," said Edward.

"Hm?" Albert answered, distracted.

Edward shrugged. "Have you ever smiled in a photograph?"

"No, have you?" asked Albert.

"Of course not."

"No. You'd look like an insane person. But I mean that . . ." Albert paused, then spoke more to himself than to Edward and Ruth. "When she smiles it's . . . I mean, even at the peak of our relationship— you know, that point when you've been with someone awhile, and you start taking it for granted, and it doesn't even occur to you that there might be a chance you could lose her—it would still completely paralyze me every time she smiled." His voice broke just a shred. "God, I love her so much."

"Oh, now I feel like I'm gonna cry," Ruth said, pulling out a lace-trimmed handkerchief.

Suddenly, Albert couldn't sit there any longer. "Let's get fucked up," he said.

The saloon was unbearably hot and stuffy, despite the fact that the night was relatively cool. It seemed as if every sweaty, foul-smelling cowboy living within ten miles of the little frontier town was packed into Old Stump's utterly inadequate recreational facility. The tired-looking old piano player poked and stabbed gamely at the keys of his decaying instrument, plunking out "Jeanie with the Light Brown Hair," his efforts barely audible over the cacophonous roar of drunken voices. A tawny whore bent lazily over the top of the piano, watching the clumsy dance of his fingers.

While it was virtually impossible for any saloon patron to avoid the crush of bodies crammed into the room, Albert's table in the far corner at least provided the relative relief of walls. It was the closest thing to privacy on offer at the only establishment in town.

Albert stared into his glass of whiskey, while Edward and Ruth watched with friendly concern. "So . . . what're you gonna do?" asked Edward.

"I dunno," Albert answered, not looking up. "Maybe I'll kill myself. I could do it out in the pasture, so the sheep could eat me. They ate a dog that died out there."

"Ew, I thought they just ate, like, grass and stuff." Edward grimaced.

"Yeah, not these," said Albert. "There's something wrong with these sheep."

Ruth put a comforting hand on Albert's. He smiled, but he subtly pulled his hand away. Not because he didn't appreciate Ruth's attempt, but rather because he knew how many local rectums her fingers had been inside. *Is it* rectums *or* recta? he wondered. *What's the plural?* Perhaps tomorrow he would ride over to the next town and see if they had a dictionary. He could look up the plural of *rectum*. That would be a fun day.

"Look," Ruth said gently, "I know things seem hopeless right now, but I promise there's a lot to live for."

Albert drained his glass of whiskey and opened the floodgates.

"Oh, really? What, Ruth? What is there to live for on the American frontier in 1882? Let me tell you something. We live in a terrible place and time. The American West is a dirty, depressing, horrible, shitty place. Everything out here that's not you wants to kill you. Outlaws. Angry drunks. Scorned hookers. Hungry animals. Diseases. Major injuries. Minor injuries. Indians. The weather. You know how Jim Wegman the blacksmith died? Wet socks."

"Come on, you're exaggerating," said Edward.

"I really am not exaggerating at all," Albert barreled on. "He went camping, he put his foot in the creek with his sock on, his foot slowly rotted, and he died. Jesus, you can get killed just by going to the bathroom! I take my life in my hands every time I walk to my outhouse! There's fuckin' rattlesnakes in the grass out there, and even if I make it, oh, hey—I can still die from cholera! You know cholera?"

"The Black Shit." Edward nodded grimly.

"The Black Shit!" Albert repeated. "The latest offering in the frontier's Disease of the Month Club."

"I heard it started with a Canadian railroad conductor," Ruth chimed in.

Albert plowed ahead. "And even if you survive all those things, you know what'll kill you? *The fucking doctor.* I had a cold a couple years ago, I went in there, and he says, 'Oh, you need an ear nail.' A *nail*. In my fucking *ear*. That's modern medicine. 'Hey, doc, I have a fever of 102.' 'Oh, you need a donkey-kickin'.' You know what else? Our pastor has shot two people. Our *pastor*."

"Really?" said Ruth.

"Yep. Shot a guy in a duel and then went and

tracked down the guy's teenage son and shot him too, 'cause he was afraid the kid would come after him outta revenge."

"Wait, how do you know that?" asked Edward skeptically.

"Because he did a *whole fucking sermon about it*!! A lesson about 'seeing things through'! Oh, by the way, here's something else: Look behind you. See those guys at that table over there? The guys who work in the silver mines? See what they're eating? Ribs doused in hot sauce."

Sure enough, three filthy-looking miners sat at a nearby table, messily gnawing away at their meals.

"That's all they eat. Did you know that?" said Albert. "They eat hot, spicy foods for every meal of the day 'cause their palates are completely dulled and desensitized from inhaling poison gas twelve hours a day. *All they can taste* are hot, spicy foods. You know what that kinda diet does to your guts? Let me tell you: constipation, cramps, dyspepsia, diarrhea, hemorrhoids, liver disease, kidney disease, bowel inflammation—they die from their own farts! Oh, and speaking of death, if you wanna see even more of that, you don't need to sit inside the saloon waiting for the inevitable shoot-out, fistfight, or full-on brawl that breaks out once a night and usually results in several deaths. No, all we need to do is step outside the front door right now!"

Strutting tipsily, Albert did his best to cut a winding pathway through the crowd, leading Ruth and Edward out through the saloon's batwing doors. He pointed across the street at a slumped-over form that lay in an alleyway next to the general store. "That is our mayor," he declared with pomp. "He is dead. He has been lying there dead for three days, and no one has done a thing: not moved him, not looked into his death, not even replaced him with a temporary appointee. For the last three days, our mayor, the highest-ranking official in our town, has been a dead guy."

Albert's eyes suddenly widened. "Oh! Oh, look! Look at that! The coyotes are dragging the body away!" Sure enough, two mangy-looking desert coyotes were tugging at the mayor's limbs with their jaws, slowly but effectively dragging the corpse farther back into the shadows of the alley.

"That is so adorable!" Albert shouted with a big drunken grin. "They're gonna feed his dick to their young! Bye, Mr. Mayor! Have fun becoming dog poop!" With that, Albert whirled around and stumbled through the batwing doors, making his way back to his chair with a red face and a spent soul.

"*That,* my friends, is the West!" he exclaimed, as Ruth and Edward joined him at the table, dutifully keeping up. "A shitty, disgusting cesspool of awfulness and despair. Fuck all of it."

"Why don't you shut up," said a sweaty cowboy at the next table, clearly tired of hearing the sheep farmer complain.

"*You* shut up," said Albert reflexively.

Twenty minutes afterward, Ruth was still dabbing at the sizable gash on Albert's forehead, which he had gotten when the sweaty cowboy flung him through the saloon window. Edward watched with concern as she dipped the already bloodied cloth back into the horse trough to moisten it. As for Albert, he was currently slumped forward in a most undignified fashion, allowing the massive amount of whiskey he'd consumed in the past ten minutes to do its holy work of spreading throughout his bloodstream and obliterating both the physical and emotional pain of the day.

"Stop it," he slurred as he swatted at Ruth's hand, knocking the reddened cloth to the dusty ground.

"Okay," she said, "But, you know, you should probably have Doctor Harper take a look at that."

Albert glared at her with undisguised derision. "Ruth, you're very sweet, but have you been listening to a goddamn thing I've been saying? You know what Doctor Harper'll say? He'll say, 'Oh, let me put a blue jay on that to peck out the blood.' Hey, wait, y'know what? You guys should have a drink with me. Let's all have a drink," he said, his bearing now flush with the confidence of a shit-faced man.

"Maybe some other time," Ruth said gently.

"I can't drink," said Edward. "When I drink, I get really vivid nightmares. I have a glass of whiskey, I fall asleep, and then within twenty minutes I dream somebody shot me in the face."

But Albert had already forgotten his own suggestion. His face was buried in his hands. "God, my life sucks," he moaned. "I miss Louise."

"Well," Ruth offered, "I don't know, maybe . . . maybe you could try talking things over with her."

Albert's head snapped upward, giving the illusion of sudden sobriety. "That's a good idea," he said. He staggered to his feet with all the stability of a sailor on the deck of a hurricane-stricken vessel.

"Wait, I didn't mean right now," Ruth said, grabbing his elbow to steady him.

Albert shook her off brusquely. "No, *right now*. That's the best time ever," he slurred.

He shuffled over to his horse, taking a roundabout figure-eight route. Curtis snorted but stood calmly and patiently as Albert made a valiant effort to get mounted. After three or four attempts, he lost his balance and thudded to the ground with one foot still tangled in a stirrup.

"Listen, Al, why don't you let us take you home," Edward said, stepping toward his struggling friend.

"No," Albert answered firmly. "No, it's okay, I just need a running start."

He ambled unevenly away from Curtis, then turned around to face the horse again. He steadied himself and barreled forward once more. He got his foot in the stirrup, leapt up over Curtis' back . . . and slid right down the other side, once again crashing into the dirt.

"Oh, God." Edward flinched. "Hey, Al, come on, you really shouldn't drink and horse."

"IgotitIgotitIgotit," Albert said. And, true to his intention, he finally managed to pull himself up onto his horse's back, where he lay on his stomach, his arms and legs dangling limply over the side. "Okay, go," he commanded listlessly, his boots spurring the animal with scant vigor. Curtis, however, knew his owner well enough to take the cue and moved off at a slow trot. Edward and Ruth could hear the receding sound of Albert's snoring as he disappeared into the night.

With a heavy heart and a heavy liver, Albert ambled toward Louise's modest white-trimmed cottage. He forced his uncooperative limbs to dismount from Curtis's back and landed unsteadily, though on his feet this time. "Okay, I'll be right back, Curtis," he slurred. "Or *not,* right? No, no, that's being too ambitious," he added, the liquor enabling him to skillfully dodge every consonant of the last word. He hugged Curtis's long equine nose with both arms. "Y'know, Curtis, we don't talk enough. We should—let's fix that. Let's fix that for sure. I love you, Curtis. I love you so much." Albert rested his head affectionately on his friend's furry muzzle . . .

. . . and woke up five minutes later in the same position, with a dribble of vomit running from the side of his mouth down toward Curtis's nostril. He straightened up with a start and wiped off the puke with his sleeve. "Oh, God, Curtis, I'm so sorry! I'm so sorry! There we go. All clean. Okay . . . here we go." Albert stumbled across the yard to the front door and gave a loud knock. He waited. There was no answer. He knocked again, even louder. After a moment, a light came on somewhere in the back of the house. He heard the padding of approaching footsteps, and Louise opened the door holding a lamp. She blinked, rubbing the sleep out of her eyes.

"Albert?"

Even unkempt and disheveled with fatigue, she was perfect. The errant strands of hair, the tangled lashes, and the reddened cheek where her head had been resting on her pillow all only served to accentuate her natural beauty. "What the hell are you doing here? It's almost 1:30," she rasped.

"Louise, we need to talk," Albert said, his consonants slippery as a wet porch.

Louise sniffed the air. "Are you drunk?" she asked.

"Oh. Yeah, well—a little. It's Curtis's birthday, so we all took him out, and . . . surprised him."

"Look, I don't know what you want from me, but it's late and I'm going back to bed." She started to close the door, but Albert thrust out an arm to stop her.

"Louise, I love you," he said. "And I know we can work this out. I know it. Just—I can be cooler. You'll see."

"Albert, no," she said sternly. "I already told you, it's over. Now—"

"I'll fight Charlie Blanche. I'll do it," he interrupted.

"I don't care about that," she sighed, losing patience.

"Can I come in?" he asked, his body swaying with intoxication. "I'm really drunk, so I'm not gonna be able to get a boner, but I want us to talk."

"Albert, get out of here," she shot back brusquely. "I don't have anything else to say to you. Listen, I'm sure you're right for somebody else, just not for me. Now, *good night*."

"Louise . . ." The drunken confidence in his expression fell away, leaving in its wake a pleading look of desperation. "What am I supposed to do without you?"

She regarded him silently for all of three seconds, then closed the door firmly.

He stood by himself, feeling like a wounded animal. "You heartless fuckin' jerk!" he shouted at the closed door, then immediately covered his bases with a heartfelt "I still love you, though!" He knew the importance of ending on a positive note.

The old prospector looked as if he'd been born a century ago. Although he was barely sixty-five, the hardship of frontier life had put its dusty, rocky foot up his ass over and over, physically aging him far beyond his actual years. His grayish-white beard was scraggly and ill-maintained, and his face was cracked and reddened from years of sun damage, with a side order of alcohol abuse. He traveled with two companions, each one seemingly as old as he was. One was his horse, a solitary old gray who dutifully pulled the little wagon with a comfortable laziness, appearing to admire the landscape as if out for a casual stroll with a favorite gal. The other was a mangy dog of no particular breed that sat next to the old man, panting and swaying back and forth in rhythm with the movement of the wagon. The dog had unkempt floppy ears and a smelly brown matting of fur, patchy and uneven courtesy of innumerable desert battles with fellow furred adversaries.

The only thing that stood out amidst this drab tableau was the object that the prospector held in his hand. It was no bigger than a golf ball, but it screamed out its presence with larger-than-life luster. It was a real, honest-to-God nugget, the first one the prospector had found in all his fifty years of scratching and pawing at the land.

He turned and gave the dog a toothy, checkered grin. "You know what I'm gonna buy you with this gold, Plugger? I'm gonna buy you a big ol' pile of fresh-cut steak."

Plugger panted happily as the old man scratched his shaggy ears.

"And I'm gonna get you a whole mess of bones fulla marrow. You like that?"

Plugger licked the prospector's liver-spotted hand.

The old man let loose a gravelly, bellowing laugh.

Plugger barked loudly in response.

The man patted the dog's mangy back. "Okay, okay, that's enough now," he said with a smile.

But Plugger's barking did not stop. Suddenly it became more intense.

"Hey, hey, settle down there, boy, whatsa matter?"

And then, as if in reply to the inquiry, the sound of approaching hoofbeats.

The prospector squinted against the bright sun. The road ahead looked empty, but the dust cloud ascending from beyond the next rise told a different story.

Riders. From the look of the dust, five or more.

His hands shaking due to both nerves and age, the old man hurriedly stuffed his glittering prize into his pocket. As he turned his attention back to the road ahead, a group of six men came galloping over the rise. The old gray shifted his weight with uneasiness, and Plugger continued his lengthy oration. As the riders approached and slowed to a stop, the old man could see that it was not six men after all. It was five men and a woman.

A rough-looking bunch too.

The lead rider was as hard-looking a man as the prospector had ever seen. The lines on his face betrayed a lifetime of anger, and the folds of his skin dove deep into those weathered grooves.

But his eyes.

Even from a moderate distance, it was evident. Those eyes were deadly. They spoke of a long-rotted soul, to which mercy and compassion had no value and never would. They were more reptilian than human, as cold-blooded as any creature that had ever lurked in the pocked depths of the Arizona desert. This was a man to be feared.

The girl was more of a puzzle. As the prospector slowed his wagon to a halt, he glanced in her direction.

She was quite beautiful. Probably mid-thirties, the old man guessed. She had a kind face, even though her stony expression was doing its best to deny the fact. Her soft-looking brown hair and graceful curves were out of place among the company she kept. She didn't belong with this group—and yet somehow she did.

Plugger's barking interrupted the old man's thoughts. "Easy, Plugger," he said. He tipped his battered hat toward the riders. "Howdy, there," he offered, his tone bright with a cheerful nonchalance he did not feel.

The lead rider spoke with a voice as calm as still water. "We'd be obliged if you could point us toward the Sherman Creek Trail."

The prospector exhaled a bit. Maybe he'd overreacted. These men were just passing through. A small band of honest cowboys heading out to Sherman Creek. Probably looking for work. Good for them. Decent work was hard to find, and if they were willing to ride that far out to make an honest day's wages, well, then, he'd be happy to point them in the right direction.

"Well, sure, I can help you there," he said.

He reached into the back of the wagon and re-trieved a tattered map. He ignored the screaming protestations of his old bones as he pulled himself down off the seat and made his way over to the lead rider. With a crooked finger he indicated a snaky black line running through the center of the map. "You're on the main road now, see? The main road goes all the way through Bullhead and then runs right into Sherman Creek Trail. But if you ask me, I'd say you'd probably get there quicker if you take Bilbee Pass. You'd be safer too. Less chance of ban-dits and such."

"Bandits?" The rider looked curious. "Are there bandits in these parts?"

"Well, I only come upon 'em a few times in my years, but you never can rightly say. Bilbee Pass is your best bet. Get you there faster too."

A smile spread across the rider's face as he stared down at the old man. But there was no warmth in it at all. In fact, to the prospector it looked less like a smile and more like a wound sliced open by the blade of an invisible swordsman.

"Thank you," the rider said, his gaze deadlocked with the milky, weary eyes of the prospector.

The old man stared back for a moment, then began backing away toward his wagon. "Oh, no trouble," he said, with a quaver in his voice. "Happy to help out a friendly stranger." The prospector prepared to pull himself up onto his wagon, when the rider spoke again.

"Oh, there's one more thing you can do for us."

The old man froze. It was a simple statement, presented calmly and courteously, nothing threatening in it at all. And yet the prospector was suddenly terrified for his life. He tried to keep the fear out of his voice as he answered. "What's that?"

"You can hand over the gold."

All pretense of civility had vanished from the rider's demeanor. The outer skin had been shed, and the reptile was poised. But for what?

The prospector somehow managed to keep his wits about him and responded with deliberate conversational passivity. "Oh, I . . . I ain't got no gold. I wish. Been prospectin' all day, and that stream's panned out. On my way back to town now."

"You see, that's just it," said the rider. "You're heading back to town in the middle of the day. Prospector only does that when he's found gold to sell. Now give it to me."

"I swear, I don't have any gold. I'm headin' into town early, cause—"

The rider drew his gun and pointed it directly at the old man's head.

The prospector no longer troubled himself to hide his terror. He could feel a warm wetness spreading around his groin. He reached into his pocket for the nugget. "Oh, now, wait a minute. Y'know, I might have a little bit of gold—"

The rider shot him in the head.

The old prospector staggered back and slumped to the ground, dead.

Plugger barked wildly, then bounded over and sniffed at his master's body with confusion.

The woman spoke for the first time, whirling angrily to face the lead rider.

"Clinch, goddammit, you didn't have to do that!"

Clinch turned and flashed his open-wound smile. "I know I didn't have to, sweetheart."

"He would've given you the gold!"

"The point is, I had to ask him twice. I'm a busy man with a schedule."

Her eyes narrowed with clear hatred. "You're a son of a bitch is what you are."

His smile vanished, and in the same instant his arm lashed out like a whip, striking her across the face with full force. She tumbled off her horse and landed hard in the dirt. Yet somehow, even as she wiped a trickle of blood from her lower lip, she managed to appear unscathed.

"Don't you ever talk to me like that again," Clinch commanded with a deadly tone. "A man's wife will show him respect. Now, let me hear you try it again."

The woman got to her feet and batted her lashes mockingly. "Oh, honey, you're the best, I'm so happy to be with you, oh, my God, I love you, I'm, like, the luckiest girl ever in the history of girls."

Before Clinch could strike her again, one of the other outlaws approached with the fallen prospector's map. "Clinch, the old man was right. We'd lose half a day goin' through Bullhead."

Clinch briefly studied the routes. He then folded the map and addressed the group of outlaws. "All right. Ben, you, Enoch, and Jordy'll ride with me. We'll follow Bilbee Pass to Sherman Creek Trail. And make no mistake about the kinda heat we're gonna draw after we take that stage. Every lawman in this territory'll be out for us." He turned to his wife, who had mounted her horse again. "And you—you're staying outta harm's way." He indicated the weasel-faced, badly scarred man mounted next to him. "Lewis, you'll ride east with Anna and hole up in this town right here." He pointed to the map. "Old Stump. We'll let things cool down, and we'll come for you in three weeks."

Anna gave Clinch a loveless smile. "Thank you so much, sweetheart, for always thinking about my safety."

He reciprocated with an even icier smile, kicked his mount, and was off. Within moments, the rest of the group was gone, and Anna remained alone save for ugly, rat-faced Lewis, a mangy dog, a tired gray horse, and the corpse of an innocent old man who had done nothing to deserve his fate.

Lewis glanced at the map and turned his horse east. "C'mon, Anna, let's go."

She began to follow him, then suddenly halted. She called out to the dog. "Plugger! Plugger, c'mon, boy!"

The dog looked up, seemingly unsure.

"C'mon, Plugger! C'mon!"

At last, thanks to the canine gift of short-term memory, Plugger came bounding after her.

They headed for Old Stump.

The days and nights rolled by, each one dissolving into the next, a chronological blur. Albert never left the house save to tend his sheep, and the tiny home's supplies and stores were beginning to run low. His mother and father clucked and barked at him to make a trip into town for replenishments, but he barely heard them. Their voices seemed to be echoing down from the rim of a deep well at the bottom of which he huddled. The rational part of his brain knew that the constant cutting pain of a breakup was only a temporary thing, that it would get a little bit easier each day, each week, each month, until one day he'd wake up and find himself utterly baffled that he had ever let this bygone woman cripple him so completely.

But that part of his brain wasn't in charge at the moment. For now he was a creature of emotion, and the suffering distorted his thinking. He lay on his bed staring up at the wooden beams on the ceiling. *I can't live without her. No one has ever loved anyone as much as I love her. And there's no one else who will ever make me as happy as she does.*

The early-afternoon sun was now lashing him across the face as it sliced through the edge of the burlap covering that hung from his window. Albert groaned in protest and turned over on his side, but he knew sleep would continue to elude him. He hadn't slept all night, and he was exhausted, but his body refused to submit to unconsciousness.

He rose sluggishly and padded into the main room. His pajamas stank from days of wear, but changing clothes had become a weekly activity, not a daily one. His mother and father sat in their usual spots, engaged in their usual activities: Elsie sewing, George reading the Bible.

"Well, look who's up at two in the afternoon," George said.

Albert stopped and stared down at him. "You ever think about reading another book, Dad? I mean, at this point, don't you pretty much know how that one ends?"

"I find new meaning in this book every day," he snapped back. "Eat something. There's still some sweet cream and pig ass on the table if you want it."

Albert glared at the unappetizing spread. "No, thanks."

"Well, you want something else? Make a run into town. This is all we got left."

Albert ignored his father and shuffled toward the front door to make an outhouse trip. When he opened the squeaky, whining door, he was startled to find Edward, mid-knock. He almost rapped Albert in the nose.

"Oh, sorry, Al."

"Edward. Hey." Albert blinked like a mole in the bright sunlight.

"My God, you look terrible." Edward frowned.

"Ahhh, there's that confidence boost I need. How *you* doin', buddy?"

"Can I come in?" asked Edward.

"Sure, sure," Albert answered with a dead expression. "I know my parents are gonna be totally thrilled to see you. Guys, Edward's here!"

George and Elsie nodded wordlessly.

"Look at them." Albert smiled without amusement. "They just love company. We all do. You want some pig ass?"

Edward shifted uncomfortably and stepped inside. "Albert, I'm really worried about you. I haven't seen you in town for a week and a half. All you do is stay home and sleep."

"Well, I went out last Tuesday to pay off Charlie Blanche so he wouldn't shoot me in the face."

"That's not what I mean."

"Look, Edward, I feel like I need to be here with my parents," Albert said, his voice dripping with the thick syrup of sarcasm. "They're not gonna be around much longer, and I wanna give back all that love and affection I got growing up. Right, Dad?"

George broke wind.

"Look," said Edward, trying to get the conversation back on track, "I know you're taking this breakup hard, and I understand . . . but I think you've got to get out of your funk. I mean, Jesus, you haven't even shorn your sheep in weeks."

"I have too," Albert shot back petulantly.

"Albert, there's a sheep out there that looks like a giant ball of cotton with legs. You can't even see its head—there's only a nose sticking out. I just saw it walk into a wall. C'mon, why don't you come into town with me, huh? We'll get a late lunch."

"Well, y'know, thank you for your concern, Edward, but if I leave the house and go into town, I might see her, and then I'm gonna get even more depressed."

"Well, of course you're gonna see her, she's in town all the time," Edward said.

Albert's head snapped upward, and he suddenly looked alert for the first time in weeks. He began to speak much more rapidly. "Why, did *you* see her? How is she? Is she sad? Did she look sad? Has she lost a lot of weight? Did she *gain* weight? Is she fat now? That would help."

"Yeah, I saw her; she seems fine," Edward answered patiently. "Which is all the more reason for you to get back out there! Show her *you're* fine too! I mean, things could be worse—"

"I'm *not* fine," Albert interrupted. "And I don't mean to sound like a jerk, but you don't know what you're talking about, okay? You have no idea what it's like. You're going home every night and having sex with your girlfriend."

"No, Ruth and I haven't had sex," Edward said matter-of-factly.

Albert stared at him for a beat, uncertain whether he'd heard correctly. "You . . . you've never had sex with Ruth?"

"No."

"You've been seeing each other for a long time, though."

"Six years. Yikes. Wow. Doesn't seem like it."

"Doesn't she . . . have sex with like ten guys every day at the whorehouse?"

"On a slow day, yeah."

Albert paused again. "But . . . *you* guys have never had sex."

"No." Edward shook his head. "Ruth says not until we're married. She's a Christian, and so am I, and we want to save ourselves for each other. Y'know, for our wedding night."

Albert allowed himself to process this information. And then he patted his friend on the shoulder. "You're right, Edward. Things could be a lot worse. I'll try to meet some people."

Albert stared at the jar of licorice. He remembered coming into the Old Stump General Store as a young boy and gazing with desire at the small but intoxicating array of three or four varieties of confections displayed on the countertop. He would ask his father for a peppermint stick or a piece of chocolate, desperately appealing to a paternally generous nature that never revealed itself. Instead, his father would say, "If you do ten hours' worth of extra chores each week for the next month, I'll buy you a peppermint stick." Albert would nod vigorously and throw himself into the task for four or five days, at which point he would inevitably decide he was getting played for a jackass. No single piece of candy was worth that much effort. So he'd give up on the whole exercise and resign himself to longing gazes. His only salvation came once a year or so, when Mr. Crawford, the now-deceased owner of the store, would take pity and offer Albert a licorice stick. The taste was euphorically sweet, but it almost made the whole ordeal worse, because it showed him what he was missing.

Now, in the prime of adulthood, the candy tortured him in a different way. He had enough of his own money to buy a piece of peppermint or chocolate, but the desire was gone. *What an ironic waste. Just another way 1882 sucks the meat.* He settled for a piece of chewing gum.

He was about to walk out with his groceries when he noticed a very pretty girl standing by the cookware, examining a pot. Had he been clearheaded and unfettered by the pain of a broken heart, he would probably have felt the stirrings of arousal, but Louise's power had snuffed out any possibility of that. Still, on a rational level, he was able to acknowledge her good looks. She had dark hair, flawless skin, and pretty brown eyes. It occurred to him that this was a perfect opportunity to take proactive control of his stagnant condition and begin the task of moving on from Louise—much as that thought made him sick to his stomach. Albert popped the chewing gum into his mouth, put on his coolest expression, took a deep breath, and walked over to the girl.

"Hi," he said.

She looked up momentarily, smiled with a polite "hello," then went back to inspecting her pot.

"I, uh . . . notice you're looking at pots," he said.

"Yeah, I am," she said, once again giving him the polite smile.

"Store's pretty great, huh?" He smiled back. "There's gotta be like twelve different items in here. I mean, how do you pick, right? It's like sensory overload." His humorous, sarcastic observation would surely get a giggle out of her.

"Yeah," she answered, offering up a less enthusiastic variant of her smile.

"Ran that eight-item store outta business. Right? That was pretty sad."

Now the girl did not respond at all. Her full attention was on the cookware.

Albert shifted his approach. "You ever tried gum?" he asked, deliberately increasing the volume of his chewing.

"No," she said, her eyes now fixed on a set of plates.

"It's this new thing, pretty cool." Albert smiled with faux confidence. "Just came out, been makin' its way around the country. It's like candy, but you don't have to swallow."

The girl put the plates back down on the shelf and granted Albert a last perfunctory look of acknowledgment. "Well, have a good rest of your day," she said, turning to the selection of fabrics farther down the shelf. Albert pretended to be very interested in a sack of henhouse feed for a moment, then moved to follow. He had one arrow left in his quiver.

"Hey, listen," he said. "I don't know if you're doing anything next Sunday after church, but they're gonna be delivering a big block of ice into town and . . . should be pretty cool to watch. You don't usually get a chance to see that much ice all together in one place."

"That doesn't interest me," she said.

"Yeah, no, me either; it's gonna be stupid," he responded, jumping ship on the idea.

Then all of a sudden she turned and looked directly at him, giving him her full attention. His courage swelled momentarily, until: "I just figured out where I've seen you," she said. "Aren't you the guy that backed out of that gunfight?"

"Uh, yeah . . . You were there?"

"Pretty much the whole town was there."

"Whole town, yeah. Guess I'm a pretty popular guy."

"No, not after that."

Knowing he'd blown this encounter and feeling defensive, Albert reverted to grade-school mode.

"Oh, yeah, like *you're* so popular," he said.

"Actually, I was voted prom queen," she responded.

"Well, okay, but . . . how many people were in your class? Like three?"

"Six."

"Oh, actually, that's a lot," he admitted.

Albert spun on his heel and walked out, feeling like shit all over again.

And so it was for the next several days. No one could have accused Albert of not trying to get back on his feet in the dating department, but between the scant offerings available in Old Stump and Albert's own romantic ineptitude, he found himself doomed to letdown after letdown.

There was young Betty Alden, the saloonkeeper's daughter, who could outdrink any man and who ended up vomiting in Albert's lap as they sat on the front porch of her home, looking at the stars. There was Georgia Behan, an attractive-enough young seamstress who, however, had a superfluous incisor growing from her left nostril, which made kissing her a painful and sometimes injurious experience. And there was Yao Ling, the lovely Chinese girl Albert had met on the road on his way back from Edward's Shoe Repair, whom he had subsequently asked out to dinner. They met at Clara's Restaurant,

Old Stump's one and only dining establishment, and it didn't take long for the evening to go sour.

"So, tell me about your family," Albert asked her as they were waiting to order. "What do your parents do?"

"Are you . . . are you serious?" she responded blankly.

"Well, yeah," Albert said.

"My dad owns a business that manufactures brass light fixtures for upscale hotels."

Albert was impressed. "Wow, really?"

Her expression instantly turned contemptuous. "No, he's a fucking railroad builder, like every other Chinaman out here."

Albert laughed nervously. "Oh. Ha. That other thing was so specific, I thought—well, I bet he's a . . . really neat guy, though," he offered lamely.

"Gosh, I wouldn't know, I never see him, " she shot back with bitterness. "You know how many hours he works?"

"Um . . . all the live-long day?"

Yao Ling was on her feet and heading out the door within seconds.

"Wait—come on!" Albert shouted desperately. "Are you . . . even allowed to be offended by any-thing I do?"

But of all his botched attempts at moving on from Louise, perhaps the most uncomfortable was the blind date. One of the neighboring dirt farmers just across the range had said he had a daughter who was still unmarried and offered to set her up with Albert. Grateful for the thought, Albert accepted and suggested a lunch meeting at Clara's. When he arrived, he found himself seated across the table from a twelve-year-old girl.

Marriage at a young age was, of course, not uncommon, but Albert wasn't the type to go in for such an arrangement. It would be difficult to maintain a satisfying, mature relationship with a woman if you were constantly being asked to help with her homework. He tried to let her down easily.

"So, I uh . . . I know this sort of thing is totally acceptable out here on the frontier, but, uh . . . not gonna lie, something about it feels kinda weird."

"My mother says I need to find a husband so I don't become an old maid," the girl said, shifting in her seat.

"Well, I . . . I think you got a few years ahead of you before that. How—how old are you?" asked Albert.

"I'll be twelve in this many days," she answered, proudly holding up eight fingers.

The waiter approached with his order pad. "Would you and your girlfriend like some dessert?" he asked.

"Oh, she's not my girlfriend," Albert answered a

little too loudly. "Um, we'll just take the check." The waiter smiled and walked away.

"Why were you such a dick about that?" The girl scowled.

"What?"

"*'She's not my girlfriend,'* " she mocked. "You were so aggressive about it. What, do I embarrass you or something?"

"No, no, but I . . ." Albert searched. "I mean, this is a first date, so I think terms like *girlfriend* are a little premature. I just want to keep this open, y'know?"

"Oh, well, I'm sorry you're feeling smothered," she said, fixing him with a cold stare.

Albert gnawed a chunk of bread. "Y'know, I'm starting to see why you don't have a husband."

The funeral was a modest affair, though certainly average by the standards of the community. It was a perfect day for it too, with the dull slate sky overhead and the chilly breeze ghosting its way across the plains. Albert and his father stood around the open grave, flanked by Edward, Ruth, and several other townsfolk. Pastor Wilson led the ceremony, reading solemnly from scripture. "O merciful God, take this good woman into thine heavenly kingdom, that she may find peace and freedom from earthly suffering," he intoned with as much life as the corpse itself.

Albert always wondered how he would feel when he lost a parent. He had assumed that George would be the first one to go, but it had turned out to be Elsie. And although she'd been in her seventies, it wasn't old age that took her. Elsie had gone outside to fetch water from the well, when a cougar attacked. The only silver lining was that the cat's initial pounce had knocked her down with such force that her skull cracked open as it slammed into a rock. Thus she was already dead when the cougar began feasting on her innards. George had rushed outside when he heard the ruckus and managed to scare the animal off with a few rounds from his Winchester, but it was too late.

And so he and Albert now stood side by side, father and son, their heads bowed low as they said their silent goodbyes to Elsie Stark, wife and mother. But although Albert felt all the pain associated with such a loss, what he felt the most was shame and confusion. *I'm more broken up over Louise than I am over the loss of my mother.* How the hell could that be? Was he so awash in self-pity and so twisted in his perspective that he'd become utterly callous to the outside world? Was he a terrible person? Or was it merely that Elsie been such a hardheaded pain-in-the-ass bitch when she was alive?

His torturous self-analysis was cut short by an empathetic hand on his shoulder.

"I'm really sorry, Albert," Edward whispered sadly.

Albert turned and offered him a polite smile of gratitude. He then turned to his father. "You okay, Dad?"

George's face was a stony-eyed mask. "She was a good solid woman," he grunted. "I liked her."

"Easy, Dad, I'm uncomfortable with all this emotion."

Two cowboys approached, each one carrying a dead body slung over his shoulder. The corpses were covered in fresh blood from multiple bullet wounds. "Hey, we got a couple more here," said the first cowboy.

"Yeah, can we get in on this grave?" said the second.

Albert sighed. "Yeah, sure." Resources were scarce on the frontier, so everyone shared what they had with the community whenever possible. The two cowboys tossed the bodies into the grave on top of Elsie, tipped their hats in appreciation, and ambled off.

Albert and Edward took their time as they strolled down the thoroughfare. They were early for church, and it was an unusually cool 92 degrees. Edward pulled out his handkerchief and dabbed at the beads of sweat on his forehead. His chunky physique didn't serve him particularly well in such a hot climate, but Albert had never heard him complain. *How the hell does he do it? He manages to find happiness in even the shittiest places.*

A young boy raced past them, deftly using a stick to guide a rolling metal hoop down the street.

"I see kids everywhere with those stick hoops lately," Albert observed.

"It's gotta be bad for their brains, right?" said Edward.

"It *has* to be. Stunts their attention spans. There was an article in the paper."

"I read that. It said it's making them unable to focus on more long-term, thought-intensive tasks."

"Exactly, it's the death of innovation. I'm telling you, when intellectual progress comes to a screeching halt twenty years from now, you can thank the stick hoop."

Suddenly Albert stopped dead in his tracks.

Halfway up the street stood the moustachery. It was a salon of sorts where a gentleman could go for a trim or a styling of his moustache. Moustaches were a sign of status and power, and the bigger, the bushier, the curlier a man's moustache, the more he was to be respected. But what paralyzed Albert was the sight of the two individuals emerging from the building. One of them was Foy Ellison, the well-groomed, well-dressed owner of the establishment.

And the other was Louise. With her arm in his.

"Ho. Ly. Shit," Albert cursed in shocked disbelief.

She had lied to him. Lied right to his face. Whether it had been in the interest of protecting his feelings or simply to avoid confrontation, he did not know. But the unpasteurized reality chewed his guts apart instantly. He hadn't thought anything could be worse than Louise leaving him, but obviously there was one thing: Louise giving herself to another man.

"Oh, God . . ." Edward shifted uncomfortably as he regarded his friend with obvious sympathy.

"She told me she didn't want to date anyone!" Albert sputtered. "She said she had to *work on herself*! Bull-fucking shit! And *Foy*! The owner of the moustachery! What. The. Fuck. If it were acceptable to be openly gay, Foy would have ten Englishmen living in his asshole."

"Maybe you should grow a moustache," Edward suggested.

"I can't afford it," Albert said with dismay. "The upkeep alone: the waxes, the oils, the creams. I don't have the cash. My God. Fucking *Foy*." Suddenly he had to be anywhere but here. "Come on, let's go. Where's Ruth? She coming to church?"

"No, she has a ten o'clock blumpkin," Edward answered matter-of-factly.

Albert stared at him, confused. "What's a blumpkin?"

"It's when a man receives fellatio while he's making stool. They just invented it in Italy, and it's become popular here." Edward smiled with pride in his awareness of world affairs.

" 'Receives fellatio'? You make it sound like a Communion service," Albert said.

"Well, it's just the process."

"So, a guy gets his dick sucked while he's taking a shit."

"Albert, don't use those words," Edward said with indignation. "It diminishes Ruth's work. She takes a lot of pride in doing a good job."

"I'm . . . I'm sorry, Edward. I wasn't thinking. It won't happen again."

"It's okay." Edward's moonfaced smile reappeared, his nature easily forgiving as always. He brightened still further as he pointed past Albert's shoulder. "Hey, look! It's the ice!"

Albert turned. Sure enough, seven men were laboring to complete the arduous task of unloading a massive block of ice from the back of a wagon. The block had endured a long journey prior to its arrival on the frontier. The Tudor Ice Company of Boston, Massachusetts, would cut large blocks of ice from frozen lakes and ponds during winter in New England and then ship them across the country, where they could be sold to communities whose climates made it impossible to otherwise acquire ice, particularly during the summer months. It was an impressive sight indeed to watch these men struggle with a block that was nearly the size of the wagon that held it. Three of them handled the rope-and-pulley system that hoisted the ice off the cart, while the other four guided it down toward the open icehouse doors, where it would be prepped for further cutting. Albert watched with fascination, allowing himself a tiny satisfied smile as he recalled the girl in the general store who had rebuffed him. "See, this is fun. She missed out."

A rope snapped. The ice fell and crushed the skull of one of the men. Thick red brain pasta spilled out into the street.

Albert and Edward screamed in horror and hurried to church.

"And make no mistake, my children," Pastor Wilson droned on in his customarily tranquilizing tone, "there shall be swift and righteous justice on all free-grazers. No more shall they nibble wantonly at the teat of our coffers. And that's just exactly like that part in the Bible that applies to that situation. Amen."

"Amen," echoed the congregation.

For the fifth time during that morning's service, Albert glanced over his shoulder as inconspicuously as he could. Louise sat on the other side of the aisle, a few rows back. Foy sat beside her. He was a classically handsome dandy, with well-oiled hair and a big cocky asshole moustache stretching out so widely on either side that it was almost like his face had two hairy arms extended in a *ta-da* gesture. *Ta-da! A colossal prick!*

As if hearing the thought, Foy glanced in Albert's direction. Albert quickly averted his gaze to the pulpit.

The pastor continued. "We would like to offer a heartfelt prayer for the family of James Addison, who was killed this morning while unloading the ice shipment. James, we'll think of you lovingly this July as we sip the cold summer beverages for which you gave your life."

Albert leaned over to Edward, whispering in disbelief, "They're still gonna use the fuckin' ice."

"Before we end the service this morning," Pastor Wilson went on, "we'd like to welcome two new members of our community: Lewis Barnes and his sister, Anna. They've just moved here to Old Stump, and they plan to build a farm, so we wish them the best of luck. That concludes today's service. God bless you for another week, and there is a mountain lion warning in effect."

As the congregation began to disperse, Albert curiously observed the new arrivals. They were an odd pair, these two siblings. The man, Lewis, looked as if God had lost a bet. His face was rough and pock-marked, his skin appearing less like flesh and more like the surface of a badly maintained dirt road peppered with horseshit. He was not a small man by any means, but his weasely, rodent-like face looked as if it belonged on a skinnier, more frail body. Albert hoped for the fellow's sake that he was either really smart or had a winning sense of humor. From the looks of him, neither was the case.

The woman was intriguing. How she could possibly be related to this guy was a mystery. She was certainly beautiful by any standard, and her face radiated a relaxed, tranquil quality that seemed too august for the hard world of the frontier. Yet as high above her dusty surroundings as she carried herself, she somehow did not seem uncomfortable with the disunion. Regardless, she would surely be over this crap town and on her way in a very short time.

The moustachery was perhaps the most well-appointed establishment in Old Stump. There were various photographs of distinguished-looking gentlemen lining the walls, each one sporting a more extravagant, flamboyant moustache than the last. There were big bushy moustaches that blocked out the lower half of the face save for the tip of the chin, thickly waxed and oiled moustaches ending in sharp spirals at either end, and moustaches that gracefully melted into fat muttonchop sideburns. This Tuesday afternoon, there were a few patrons scattered about the place. One sat comfortably in the grooming chair, getting a moustache trim; another examined an array of waxes, oils, and creams; a third was engaged in conversation with Foy himself.

"I would say you could try oiling it into a fine curl," Foy suggested, rubbing his thumb and forefinger together for emphasis. "Your moustache definitely has the body for it."

"Yeah, I've thought about that, but I sorta like it a little messy, y'know? Sorta fun?" the customer answered with a conflicted tone.

"Well, if that's what you're going for, I'd use the cream, and I would definitely let it grow."

"See, I kinda wanna do that."

"And, you know what, I see the hesitation on your face, but, trust me, you could do that."

"Like shoulder length?"

"Do it. You'll thank me."

"See, I've always wanted to do shoulder length, but I'm worried I don't have the chin for it."

"You have the chin for it," Foy assured him.

"Okay, wow, you just gave me, like, a whole bunch of confidence."

"Try the cream for a few weeks, and let me know how it goes."

"I will, thank you. I'm excited now! I want it to grow really fast!" The man hurried out the door.

As it swung back, Louise gracefully sauntered in, all bouncing blond curls and coquettish smiles for her wealthy new boyfriend. "Hi!" She beamed, throwing her arms around him.

"Hey, you." Foy grinned. He grabbed her by the waist and kissed her long and hard. She reciprocated momentarily, then pulled away as she swung her hips back and forth, flashing her most seductively girlish smile.

"So, the fair's coming up soon, and I thought maybe we could go dress shopping later," she said, batting her long lashes.

Foy took the cue. "You know, I was thinking you could use a new dress."

"Something . . . expensive?" she said, sliding a slender white finger down the center of his chest.

"Stupidly expensive," he said, his tone theatrically devilish.

She laughed gaily and reached a hand around the back of his neck, pulling him in for another kiss.

Albert was just in time to get an eyeful as he walked through the door. Yes, he'd had time to process the breakup. Sure, he'd tried to move forward by seeing other people. Yes, he'd known Louise and Foy were together. But the actual sight of her kissing him was a knife in his side. And suddenly all the agony came surging back in a nauseating wave, and he hurt all over again just as much as the day he'd lost her. But he'd be damned if he'd let it show.

Foy saw him first, and quietly pulled his lips away from his new girlfriend's.

Louise turned to look and immediately lowered her gaze with an embarrassed sigh. "Oh, Jesus," she muttered under her breath.

"Hi, Albert," Foy greeted him confidently.

"Hello," Albert answered, warily stepping inside. He pretended to be disinterested as he surveyed the various moustache-related products lining the shelves.

"What's up, kiddo?" said Foy. "Never seen you in here before."

"Just, um . . . browsing." Albert hoped his faux nonchalance was at least somewhat convincing.

"Yeah . . . you don't have a moustache, though."

"Well, I was . . . I was thinkin' about growin' one."

Louise whispered to Foy, loud enough for Albert to hear, "I'm gonna use the powder room." She whirled with spinning skirts and retreated through a door in the back.

Albert felt another stab of distress. He'd shared so much love with this girl, so many good times, so many memories . . . and now she couldn't even bear to be in the same room with him. Again, he managed to conceal his piercing heartache and kept his attention on Foy.

"What kinda moustache you looking to grow?" Foy asked, taking a couple of steps toward Albert.

"Um . . . a big one." Albert suddenly had no clue at all why he'd even set foot in this place or what he'd hoped to accomplish. "The kind that . . . goes down below my mouth, and then along the edge of my jaw . . . and then, um . . . goes up and becomes my sideburns, and then becomes my hair."

"A Möbius moustache," said Foy without missing a beat.

"A Möbius moustache, yeah," Albert responded, acting as if it had been on the tip of his tongue the whole time.

As if sensing Albert was in over his head, Foy doubled the condescension in his tone. "You know, that sort of moustache is a costly facial accessory."

"Yeah," said Albert with false assuredness.

"Well . . . you're a sheep farmer." Foy grinned a grin that made Albert wish cholera upon him.

Fuck it. "You feel good about what you're doing?" Albert said, taking a step closer to the moustachier.

Foy appeared unbothered. "What am I doing?"

"Stealing a guy's girlfriend?" Albert could feel his face getting red with both fury and embarrassment. "You able to sleep at night?"

"Hey, Louise dumped *you,* my friend. It's not my fault she wanted someone with more to offer. I can give her a lavish home. Warm blankets. Wrapped candies. Can you say the same, Albert? Can you give Louise wrapped candies?"

Albert locked gazes with him for a moment. "Fuck you, man," he blurted, knowing he'd lost this round and feeling dumb as a mule.

"Yeah, that's what she's doing," Foy shot back, finishing the match. Albert stormed out of the moustachery in defeat, resolving never to return. Not to this establishment, and not to Old Stump. It was time to go.

That evening Edward sat patiently at a corner table in the Old Stump saloon, nursing a beer. He really wasn't much of a drinker. Drinking, he supposed, was for the unhappy. For those who wished to block out the misery of their lives. Edward felt no such dissatisfaction. He derived great pleasure from his work as a cobbler, he adored his little apartment just above the workshop, and, most of all, he was over the moon with happiness in his blissful relationship with Ruth. He smiled to himself, knowing that in just a few minutes she'd be finished having sex with the pastor's son upstairs in the brothel, and then she'd come bounding down those steps with a big kiss for her devoted boyfriend. He wanted to be sure he was church-sober for that sweet confection.

As Edward took another baby sip from his mug, he observed Old Stump's two newcomers entering through the batwing doors and making their way over to the bar. *Anna and Lewis Barnes,* they were called. New faces were always welcome as far as Edward was concerned, the continued growth of the town being of great value and importance to everyone.

At last, Ruth came hurrying down the stairs and made her way over to Edward's table. She looked disheveled and unkempt, but Edward saw none of it. He saw only what he always saw: the most beautiful woman in the world, and the purest, most magnificent representation of true love that any man could ever hope for. He kissed her eagerly as she sat down.

"Hi, honey!" he said with a warm smile.

"Oh, gosh, that was a long day." She sighed, sinking into the chair and helping herself to a generous draught of his beer.

"Aw, what happened?"

"This guy wanted me to smoke a cigar and ash on his balls while I jerked him off."

"Really? Wow, see, your job is interesting 'cause no two days are alike," he said with envy. "I go to work and I'm, like, grrr! Monotony!"

"Yeah, I guess it'd be worse if I was at a desk all day," she agreed. "That's why I love you, sweetie. You can always find the silver lining in everything."

"I love you too," he said, taking her hand. He gazed into her eyes for a long moment. "Ruth, honey, I've been thinking."

"About what?"

"Well . . . you know how much we love each other."

"With all our hearts," she said sweetly, kissing his fingers.

"And we've been together a long time, and . . . well . . . what do you think about . . . us spending the night together?"

Ruth looked thunderstruck. "You mean . . . sharing a bed?"

"Yes."

"And . . . having sex?"

"Well, I mean, not right away. We could just lie

together the first few times, see how it feels, and then go from there."

"Eddie," she said, her tone suddenly quite serious, "we're Christians."

"I know we are. And I want to do the correct thing in the eyes of the Lord, but if we really love each other, then wouldn't God be okay with it?"

"Honey, I don't know—you're talking about premarital relations," she said, glancing away as she processed the enormity of what he was proposing.

As she turned, he noticed a small dollop of semen trickling down her left cheek. "Oop, you got a little somethin' there," he said, taking out his handkerchief and dabbing gently at the milky fluid.

"Thanks." She smiled. "But, Eddie, I . . . God, I'm not sure it'd be right."

"Okay. I understand. But maybe think about it?"

Before she could answer, Albert came barreling over to the table and sat down with a defeated expression.

"I'm out," he declared.

"Huh?" said Edward.

"I'm out. I'm gone. I'm getting outta here, and I'm going to San Francisco."

"What?" Ruth looked at him with concern.

"Yeah, I just wanted to say goodbye."

"Whoa, whoa, Al . . . are you serious?" Edward

asked with a furrowed brow. "Is this because of Louise?"

"Yes, I'm fucking serious. There's nothing but shit for me here, and I'm out. I hate the frontier, I hate everything in it, I'm done."

And then all hell broke loose.

It started over at the bar, where rat-faced Lewis had ordered a shot of whiskey. As he lifted the glass to his lips, a young cowboy standing directly behind him threw his head back and let out a bellowing guffaw, presumably over some joke told by one of his cohorts. The back of his head knocked against Lewis's. Not hard, but just enough to send the drink spilling out of the glass and all over Lewis' shirt. The young cowboy, obviously already inebriated, whirled around with a bellicose glare.

"Hey, watch it, pal!" he barked, exhaling smoke from his cigarette directly into Lewis's face.

Lewis did not flinch. "I think you owe me a drink, fella."

The cowboy laughed derisively. "Like hell I do. You best watch where you stand."

Lewis moved an inch closer. He was slightly smaller than the other man but somehow appeared far more threatening. "I don't think you heard me," he said softly. "I'm thirsty."

"Well, then, go down to the river and take a dunk."

Lewis narrowed his eyes. "Last chance, kid."

The young cowboy regarded him for a beat, appearing to register the severity in Lewis's gaze. He picked up an empty shot glass, poured a fresh shot of whiskey, and handed it politely to Lewis. Lewis accepted it graciously, even hoisting the glass a bit in apparent acknowledgment of the peace offering. Then, as Lewis lifted the whiskey to his lips, the young cowboy grinned widely and dropped his lit cigarette into the glass.

Lewis looked down at the gray ash floating in the amber fluid, promptly drew his gun, and fired. The young cowboy was dead in seconds.

His friends wasted no time. One of the other men grabbed the nearest bottle off the bar and smashed it across Lewis's head. Blood streamed from his face as he tore furiously at the shards of glass jutting out of his ruined flesh.

"That was my bottle, you son of a bitch!" somebody shouted, and in an instant, the entire saloon erupted like a volcano. Dirty, sweaty, drunk men began to indiscriminately swing roundhouse punches at one another, breaking chairs, glasses, bottles, and anything else they could get their hands on.

"Oh, shit!" Albert cried, bolting to his feet. "Why the fuck does this always have to happen?! Two guys get in a fight and then suddenly we all have to start fighting!"

"C'mon, hurry, get in position!" Edward exclaimed as he grabbed Albert and pulled him into the corner. They fell into it, as they had countless times before: an animated flurry of pretend punches thrown furiously at each other, while being very careful never to make contact. The idea was that, as long as they appeared to be brawling along with everyone else, neither one of them would make an easy target for any genuine violence.

"Ooh! Ow! We got our own thing going on over here!" shouted Edward.

"Yeah, and it's really bad! Ouch, stop fighting me!" Albert hollered back.

"Ow, this is so intense over here!"

"Yeah, nobody needs to get in on this! We're both getting hurt pretty bad!"

One of Edward's punches accidentally connected.

"OW!" Albert yelped, with a sizable flinch.

"Oh, my God, I'm so sorry!" cried Edward.

"You actually hit me!"

"Albert, I'm really sorry, I didn't mean to."

"Do I have a mark?"

"Yeah, there's a little redness there."

"Yeah, it feels like it."

"You want a moist rag?"

Before Albert could respond, something caught

his eye across the room. On the upper level near the brothel, two cowboys were pummeling each other fiercely. One clearly had the advantage as he delivered blow after blow, sending his opponent crashing against the wooden railing. It began to crack. Albert could not have cared less about the destruction of saloon property, but what did concern him was Anna Barnes, the newcomer. She stood just below the upper level, surveying the fray with an oddly detached look in her eye, almost like a disapproving mother watching her children scuffling in the mud, ruining their Sunday clothes. The slugfest continued directly above her, and Albert watched with alarm as the railing began to collapse. Without thinking, he broke free of his make-believe fistfight with Edward and sprinted straight through the center of the mêlée toward the opposite end of the room.

Miraculously, all he got was a stray elbow in the ribs and a splash of beer in the eye before he reached Anna Barnes. He grabbed her arm and yanked her out of the way as hard as he could, just as the battered cowboy above came crashing down from the upper level, bringing a hailstorm of heavy wooden debris along with him.

Anna turned and looked at Albert with surprise. She opened her mouth to speak, but before she could say a word, a whiskey bottle flew past her face, shattering against the wall inches from her head.

"Come on!" Albert yelled, pulling her along with him by the wrist as he scurried out through the batwing doors. The two of them half-ran, half-stumbled out into the evening air and the relative safety of the dusty thoroughfare.

Anna turned to Albert. "Thank you," she said.

It was the first time he'd heard her speak, he noted, and she had a pleasant alto quality to her voice. Even from two words, he was aware of her markedly undisturbed reaction to what had been a potentially traumatizing close call. She didn't appear shaken or out of breath in any way whatsoever. Albert, for his part, was heaving with the aftershocks of panic as he bent over to brush the dust off his trousers.

BANG! BANG!

He jolted upright, just in time to see Sheriff Arness and his deputy racing into the saloon, guns blazing into the air.

"Let's get the fuck outta here," he said with a resurgence of agitation. The two of them made their way up the street, away from the chaos.

Neither said anything for a while. Albert was painfully aware that this woman was giving him time to collect himself before she struck up any kind of a conversation. He felt silly. She'd been the one in danger, and yet she seemed utterly at ease. Meanwhile, his hands were still shaking.

"Nice work back there," she remarked at last. "I guess you're a real hero, huh?"

"Oh, no, I'm not the hero," he answered with a flushed face. "I'm the guy in the crowd making fun of the hero's shirt."

She gave a small chuckle, which was promptly interrupted by a loud bark. Plugger came bounding out of the darkness and happily fell into step beside Anna, giving her hand a friendly lick.

"Hey, look who's here." She smiled. "This is Plugger."

"Oh, hey, Plugger," Albert said, gamely scratching the mangy dog's head. He turned and regarded Anna with a look of curiosity. "So . . . that was your brother, huh?"

"Lewis, yeah." She rolled her eyes.

"Uh-huh. Does he generally commit murder over beverage-related disputes?"

"He's always been a little rambunctious."

"Yeah, he seems like a character," Albert deadpanned. "You're okay, though?"

"Oh, I've seen him do it a hundred times. I don't have to worry about Lewis, he'll pull himself out no problem."

"Well, that's . . . that's good, I guess. I'm, uh . . . I'm Albert, by the way," he said, offering a hand.

She shook it firmly. "I'm Anna. Nice to meet you, Albert."

"So, you guys just got into town, huh? Welcome to our awesome town," he said, grandly extending an arm to show off the unremarkable shithole that was Old Stump.

"Thanks." She smiled. "Lewis and I moved here from Kansas City."

"Kansas, huh?"

"No, it's in Missouri."

"Oh, right. That's annoying and weird."

"Yeah, we were wanting a change, so we came out to the frontier looking to build a farm." Plugger jabbed at her leg with his nose, a dry stick hanging out of his mouth. She plucked it from his jaws and tossed it farther up the thoroughfare. The dog scurried after it with clumsy urgency.

"Really? I'm a farmer myself," he said without pride or enthusiasm. "I have a farm about two miles from here."

"Oh. Cattle?"

"Sheep."

"Ah."

"Yeah."

"Well, that's gotta be fulfilling work, right?" she asked, plainly hearing the dolefulness in his voice.

"It's great," he answered flatly. "It's like being a dog walker for a hundred and fifty really stupid dogs."

She laughed openly for the first time. "It can't be that bad. Sheep are cute."

"That's the problem. I mean, if I was a cattle farmer, that'd be one thing, y'know? That's a manly job. You use cows to make beef. Leather. Tough things. With sheep you make sweaters. I'm basically a sweater farmer."

"That's good; we're all hoping for a bountiful sweater harvest this year."

Their stroll came to a halt as they reached the fat, ugly tree stump that jutted up from the ground smack in the center of the thoroughfare. "I'm assuming this is why the town is called Old Stump," Anna said.

"Yeah, this is it." He sighed with boredom. "When they built the town, they had to cut down this big tree, but they couldn't move the stump. They didn't have any dynamite and they ran out of black guys, so they had to leave it here, right in the middle of the street."

"Well, why couldn't they just build the town fifty feet that way?" she asked, pointing off to her left.

Albert stared at the stump. No one had ever asked that question before. It was a very good question. He thought it best to move on. "So, why would you leave Kansas City for the Western frontier?" he asked. "I mean, it sucks out here."

"I don't know—it's exciting," she said, with a bright, attentive gaze, as if seeing a completely different town than he was. "Everything's so new and unpredictable."

"Well, that is true, nothing is what it seems. Like, look—see that building right there? We have no idea what's inside. I mean, it could be *anything*. This whole place has such an air of mystery about it." He gave her his best wide-eyed impression of awe-struck curiosity as he pointed to a shabby structure with the single word BANK painted on the front.

Anna laughed again. "I'm getting the sense that you're kind of a negative guy."

"Well, Jesus, look where I live," he grumbled. "Oh, hey, here's a fun fact about the American West in 1882. You receive the same punishment whether you're a horse thief or a retarded newborn."

"They hang retarded newborns?"

"Yep, as a warning to others. I shit you not." He sighed. "But none of it is my problem anymore. I'm leaving tomorrow."

"Really? Where are you going?"

"San Francisco. You know, civilization. A place where you're not taking your life in your hands in eight different ways just by walking to the outhouse to shit."

"Well, you gotta do what makes you happy, I guess." She shrugged.

"Happy is a tall order," he said, staring off toward the moonlit mesas in the distance, "but at least this'll make me not dead."

She studied his face for a moment, and he became acutely aware of being sized up by an expert. "Could it be," she asked with raised eyebrows, "that you are also a man with a broken heart?"

A man who's been through a recent breakup will seize on any and every opportunity to relive his misery by telling his story to anyone who will listen, and Albert was no different. Perhaps it was because he secretly hoped that eventually, if he spread the word far and wide enough, someone would emerge with a magic bullet of sorts: that one piece of sage counsel, that one solution he hadn't thought of, that one thing that could fix his life and get Louise back.

He grabbed ahold of the moment. "Since you brought it up, can I unload all my shit on you?"

She smiled. "Well, I do owe you one."

From high up on the ridge, the lonely, ramshackle town of Old Stump appeared almost idyllic. It lay nestled below them, just a few soft orange lights glowing amidst the vast darkness of the cold desert night. Albert and Anna sat on a wide rocky outcropping, a spot that Albert had been coming to since he was a little boy. He called it the "swearing place." When he was a child, his mother and father had been strict Puritans who would not tolerate any foul language inside the house. So Albert would save up his cuss words till the end of each week, write them all down on a sheet of paper, then climb to the top of the ridge and shout them across the plains as loud as he could. It was perfectly cathartic, and he always felt better after screaming a mouthful of obscenities out at the hot, depressing frontier he loathed so very much.

"I did everything in the world for her," he said, picking absently at a handful of dead grass. "If she was happy, I was happy. That's all I cared about. I was generally broke, but I'd save every scrap of extra income just to buy her gifts as often as I could: a bouquet of roses, a new bonnet, a bottle of perfume, anything to remind her as often as possible how important she was to me and how much I loved her. She was the one thing that made the shootings and the wild animals and the Indians and the disease and the general depressing awfulness of the West somehow bearable."

"How did you and Louise meet?" asked Anna.

"We both had dysentery in the same hospital."

"Oh."

Albert allowed himself a sad smile at the tender recollection. "I was over in Sherman Creek for a few days buying sheep stuff, and that's when the out-break hit. Leveled me for a week straight. I checked in to the hospital, and when they assigned me to a bed, I found that I'd been placed next to the most beautiful woman I'd ever seen in my life. God, even in a sweaty, feverish diarrhetic state, Louise was an absolute vision. She'd lived in Sherman Creek her entire life, and somehow we'd never crossed paths. Well, we talked and talked for a week—there was nothing else to do—and after only a few days it seemed like we'd known each other our whole lives. And I'll tell you, what's really special about the whole thing is that . . . you know how when you've been in a relationship with someone for a while and you're so comfortable that it doesn't even matter if the other person sees you going to the bathroom? Well, this was the reverse, because our relationship *started* with us shitting blood in front of each other. And that bonds people. So she came back to Old Stump with me, I helped her get set up with a job as a schoolmarm, and she's been here with me ever since."

"She a good marm?"

"She can marm. She can definitely marm. And the whole time we were together, I thought, *I'm so* happy. *How can I* possibly *be this happy? One of these days she's gonna figure out she's too good for me*. And then . . . one day she did." Albert let the dead grass fall from his hands. "I finally tricked one girl into falling in love with me, and I lost her."

Anna regarded him as she digested the tale. The pain in his voice was unmistakable, and yet there was something missing from the equation.

"Look, obviously I don't know all the details," she said, "but from what you've told me . . . I think you got this whole thing upside down. I mean, it sounds like you've had this girl on a pedestal and treated her like a queen. You've clearly bent over backward for her, but what's she given you back?"

Albert seemed baffled by the question. "I told you, she made me happy in an otherwise rotten world. I mean, if someone can do that . . . well, they *deserve* to be on a pedestal."

"Do you really want to go to San Francisco?"

"Yes, I—no. I don't know," he said. "I guess I don't. I want . . . I just want Louise." His voice broke ever so slightly on the last word.

"Uh-huh." Anna nodded, accepting the shape of his predicament at face value for the moment. "Well, if this Foy guy is that much of a douche, she'll figure it out if she's smart. Sometimes a girl has to get a few assholes out of her system before she realizes what a good guy looks like." She patted him gently on the arm.

And then they heard the rattle.

Albert froze. The sound had come from his left. He slowly looked down and saw it slithering between his foot and Anna's. It was practically touching his shoe. "Oh, fuck," he said softly.

"That's a diamondback, isn't it?" she said in an equally hushed tone, but with a surprising degree of calmness.

"Yeah, it is."

"Well, fuck."

"If we hold still, we'll be fine."

The snake slid across the tip of Albert's foot. He held his breath. Deadly poisonous snakes were naturally to be feared out here on the frontier, but there was also something about them that Albert found infuriatingly arrogant. The way they showed up out of nowhere and put everyone's whole goddamn life on hold for minutes at a time, striking mortal terror into the hearts of people who were just minding their own business. A man would stand, immobile as a statue, in fear for his life while the snake writhed around aimlessly, taking its sweet time, and not giving a fuck about anybody but itself.

"Asshole," Albert muttered.

"Huh?" said Anna.

"Nothing." At last, the diamondback wound its way past their little outcropping and slithered off into the darkness. Albert and Anna exhaled with relief.

"So, you're really leaving tomorrow, huh?" she asked, casually picking up where they'd left off.

"Yeah. Tomorrow."

"Why don't you at least stay through the weekend? Isn't the fair on Saturday?"

"Oh, fuck that," Albert snorted. "Louise is gonna be there, and she's gonna be with Foy. No way. I'm not putting myself through that."

"Well, then, I'll go with you," she offered. "I haven't really made any other friends since I've been in town, and I could sure use some fun. Besides, there's no better way to make your ex-girlfriend want you back than to have her see you with another girl."

Albert silently acknowledged the truth of that statement. He sighed. "Maybe."

"Especially a smokin'-hot girl." She grinned. "She sees me, she'll be intimidated as fuck."

"Oh, you're very modest, I see," said Albert, warming up a bit.

"Yes, I'm a little cocky, but with these tits I can afford to be."

For the first time in weeks, Albert Stark laughed.

BAR BRAWLER ARRESTED FOR MURDER, the headline read. Not that the toothless old man was interested in the story. The newspaper lay draped across

94

his upper body and face, shielding him from the vicious morning sun as he snored peacefully in front of the sheriff's office. He didn't notice the slender shadow that glided over him as Anna passed through the doorway.

Sheriff Arness sat at his desk, whittling some sort of unidentifiable animal out of a small block of wood. Whether it was a horse or a duck, Anna couldn't tell. The sheriff stopped his whittling and looked up as she approached.

"Can I help you, ma'am?"

"Yes, I'm here to see my brother," she said, her words heavily weighted with a tone of disgust.

"Oh, yeah, the Barnes boy," the sheriff said, putting aside his feeble attempt at sculpture and rising from his seat. "You know, he's in a lotta trouble."

"I know." She rolled her eyes. "He's an idiot who can't control his temper, and I apologize for that. Seems like every town we visit, he winds up behind bars over some brawl or other."

"Well, he picked the wrong town and the wrong brawl," the sheriff said gravely. "The man he killed is Pastor Wilson's son. Pastor Wilson's a popular man around these parts, but that ain't the half of it. His cousin is married to one of them congressmen back east. If I had to bet on it, I'd say there's gonna be a hangin'."

Anna took a moment to process this. *I'm not cer-*

tain I could feel sorry for him even if he were actually my brother, she thought. "Can I speak with him?" she asked. Sheriff Arness nodded and got up from his chair. He led her over to a row of three cells lined with brown, rusty bars. In the middle one, Lewis lay sleeping on a small yellowed cot. The sheriff rattled the creaky bars. "Barnes! Wake up; you got a visitor."

Lewis's eyes fluttered open. When he saw Anna, he slowly rose to his feet with a scowl. His face was still a mess from the broken bottle. Clearly the doctor had paid him a visit, but the wound dressings looked somewhat inadequate.

Anna turned back to the sheriff. "Do you mind if I have a moment alone with him?" she asked.

"Go right ahead," he replied, seemingly eager to return to his whittling.

Anna stared at Lewis. "You dumb asshole," she said softly.

"Shut up," he barked. "I didn't know who he was. And besides, he was all up in my face, you saw—"

"You shot the pastor's son. You realize they're probably gonna hang you."

Lewis moved closer to the bars and lowered his own voice. "Oh, is that what they're sayin'? Well, who gives a fuck? When Clinch gets in to town, it's not gonna matter *what* they do. He'll bust me out, and anyone who tries to stop him is gonna be a dead man."

"You know something?" she said, starring him down with conviction. "One of these days there's gonna be a man who's faster than Clinch. And stronger. And smarter. And then Clinch is gonna be the dead man. And I'm gonna smoke a big, fat fucking cigar to celebrate."

Lewis took another step closer to the bars. Anna did not step back. "I don't think Clinch would like you talkin' about him that way," he said, his eyes narrowing. "Not a nice thing for a man's wife to say about her husband."

"Well, we'll see if he gets here in time, huh?" she said, a hint of a smile creeping into her expression. "Tick tock."

His hand lashed out at her, but she moved swiftly out of its reach with a ballerina's grace. She whirled around and was gone.

The fairgrounds bustled and buzzed with the once-a-year gathering of visitors from three different towns: Sherman Creek, Bullhead, and Old Stump. The result of the aggregation was a crowd of a size rarely seen in these sparsely populated regions of the frontier. Merchants cried their wares, bakers and cooks displayed all manner of elaborate confections, and barkers hollered and gesticulated as they attempted to lure passersby toward the games, contests, magicians, and exotic animals that peppered the normally barren desert landscape. It was an uncomfortably hot day as usual, and Albert wiped his soaking-wet forehead with his sleeve as he rode up to the entrance. As he reined in and dismounted, he heard a familiar shuffling sound behind him.

Baaa! Baaaa!

He turned around just in time to see two of his sheep hurrying to catch up.

"Oh, Jesus," he muttered. "Did you guys follow me all the way from home? No! Get outta here! Go home! Jonathan! Andrew! Go!" The sheep stared at him with puzzled looks on their fluffy faces, before reluctantly turning and awkwardly shuffling back in the other direction. Albert sighed as he tethered Curtis to a wooden hitching post.

"Hey, sheepboy!" a familiar voice called out.

Albert turned to see Anna trotting up on a brown horse that almost matched the color of her hair. She wore a light-green dress with a white flower pattern, and her hair was down, the curly locks spilling over her shoulders in a carefree yet elegant fashion. She'd worn it up the night of the saloon brawl, and Albert observed that she looked decidedly more feminine today. She greeted him with a broad smile.

"Hey." He waved to her, wondering how anyone with a sibling who had recently been arrested for murder could be in such apparent high spirits. "Jesus, I heard about your brother," he said. "Are you okay?"

"I'm fine," she answered, dismounting from her horse. "And, Albert, do not worry about Lewis. Anything that happens to him right now is his own fault. Got it?" The lightness in her tone was undeniable. She really didn't seem to be bothered at all.

Albert shrugged, deciding not to press the matter. "Yeah, sure," he said.

"Good!" She playfully tipped his hat forward over his eyes. "'Cause you know what I wanna do?"

"Um . . . eat hot food in hundred-degree weather?"

"No." She laughed. "Get my picture taken. I've never done it before."

"That's horseshit."

"It's the truth."

"No, I mean, that's horseshit. Be careful."

They sidestepped the mound of equine leavings.

"Come on, let's go!" Anna grabbed his hand, and he almost face-planted in the dirt as she broke into a run, pulling him toward the busy fairground.

They made their way through the excited, perspiring throng toward a painted wooden sign reading PHOTOGRAPHS! MADE BY LIGHTNING AND GOD HIMSELF! Albert had had his photograph taken only a few times in his life, but the technology always intrigued him. He watched as a family of six clustered together in front of the large wooden camera.

The photographer huddled under the black covering. "Okay, everybody hold still!" he instructed. The family stood expressionless as the photographer held up the flashlamp. After a beat, there was a loud *pop* as the fuse ignited the explosive magnesium powder, momentarily illuminating the rigid, stone-faced subjects. Albert watched the wisps of residual smoke dissipate in the air.

Anna turned to him. "Y'know, supposedly there's some guy in Texas who smiled one time while he was getting his picture taken."

"Shut the fuck up," Albert blurted with excitement. "I was talking about that just the other day! Are you serious?"

"I think. I mean, I heard it somewhere. I dunno if it's true."

"Yeah, that sounds like the kinda bullshit somebody would make up." They took their place in line as a dirt farmer and his wife stepped in front of the photographer's camera. A vendor walked past, selling some sort of snack that looked like barbecued meat on a stick. Realizing he was hungry, Albert fished a penny out of his pocket and bought one.

"So." Anna smiled. "We know what kind of girl you like. What kind of girl do you *not* like?"

"Huh?"

"Like, what's the *worst* quality for you in another person?"

"Oh, that's an interesting question." Albert smiled as he bit into the meat. He chewed twice, immediately registered that it tasted like fermented dog shit, and spat it onto the ground.

Anna continued. "That deal-breaker thing that you absolutely cannot tolerate. For me it's tobacco-chewing. I don't care how much a guy smokes, but if he chews, forget it. There's no way I'm kissing that. And he's definitely not going down on me."

"Wow, that's beautiful," said Albert. "You should stitch that into a pillow."

"Oh, I have. It's embroidered all fancy and it says, *Don't go snackin' if you been tobaccin'*."

Albert couldn't help but laugh.

Anna smiled and continued to press him. "What about you?"

He debated whether to be honest about this one, but there was something about Anna that made him feel like he could let his guard down a bit. "Um . . .

well, you're gonna think this is fucked up, because it is, but . . . I really can't handle it when a girl looks like her dad."

"Okay, that's bizarre. Why?"

"Well . . . I mean, if I'm dating a girl, and then I meet her mom and dad, and it turns out she looks like him, and I see all the matching facial features and the bone structure and whatnot, from then on every time I kiss her, I'm very aware that I'm kissing the dad's facial geography."

"I see."

"Yeah," he continued. "I was dating this girl about ten years ago, and she and her family and I all went down to the creek for a swim one day, and her dad took his shirt off, and he had the exact same nipples as she did. I had to move to a different town for a while."

She took a beat. "I'm surprised your girlfriend left you."

Albert took the jab with a laugh.

By now they were next in line for a photograph, following a young couple in their early twenties. "Okay, hold still," the photographer called out. He pushed the electric fuse, and the magnesium flash powder exploded. The young couple and the photographer were all killed instantly, their bodies blown to pieces and charred beyond recognition.

Albert and Anna quickly scurried backward and

away from the calamity as clusters of fairgoers scrambled to retrieve buckets of water. "Jesus Christ!" Albert exclaimed. "This fucking fair! Every year something happens and, *boom*! People die."

"Really?" Anna said, sounding almost as shaken as Albert.

"Last year there were two gunfights, a stage collapsed, there were two knife fights, a drowning, and the Indians attacked."

"God, why are the Indians always so mad?" she wondered.

"I don't know."

"I mean, we're basically splitting this country fifty-fifty with them."

"They're just selfish."

They made their way deeper into the fairgrounds, where more barkers could be heard shouting over one another, each doing his best to compete for the attentions of the passersby.

"Sir! Sir and madam! May I divert your attention over here for a moment!" The weathered-looking peddler at the small kiosk appeared to be selling all manner of tonics, elixirs, powders, and salves. His eyes widened with eager delight as he registered Albert and Anna's approach. He instantly set about arranging a display of his finest samples on the table in front of him. "Welcome, welcome! Can I interest you in a miracle cure? Only the finest healing tonics and elixirs procured from the farthest corners of the globe!" He presented Albert with a small green bottle.

Albert read the label. *"Ogden's Celebrated Stomach Bitters."* He looked up at the peddler. "Can I . . . can I just ask—celebrated by whom? Who's celebrating stomach bitters?"

Anna took the bottle and turned it around to read the back. "God, look at the ingredients," she said, wrinkling her nose. "Alcohol, cocaine, morphine, mercury with chalk—what the hell is *mercury with chalk?*"

"Science!" The peddler grinned with a theatrical flourish.

Albert continued reading the ingredients. "And red flannel. *Red flannel?* There's *shirt* in here?"

"Pieces of shirt," the peddler said with enthusiasm.

"Okay, thank you." Albert handed the bottle back to him, offering a polite smile as he and Anna stepped away.

The peddler desperately grabbed another bottle, holding it up as he called after them. "Would you care to try some Parker's Liquid Beef Tonic?"

Albert sighed. "You'd think these guys would know everybody's caught on to the fact that it's all just booze with fancier labels and—" He stopped in his tracks. "Oh, God."

"What?" asked Anna.

"That's them."

Just ahead, strolling arm in arm and looking like bliss incarnate, were Louise and Foy. She sipped a glass of lemonade with a look of utter contentment on her face, as Foy whispered something in her ear. She turned and graced the moustachier with a smile so adoring that Albert's heart plunged suicidally from his chest into the pit of his stomach. To make matters worse, there was no way to pass the two of them without being noticed.

Albert frantically grabbed Anna's elbow. "Shit, here they come! Quick, let's pretend you just said something funny." Albert had already burst into loud, uproarious laughter before he realized he'd fucked up. "Wait, no—shit! *You* pretend *I* just said something funny!"

Anna grinned at him. "Come on, introduce me," she said, taking his arm and pulling him forward.

"No!" he whispered frantically. "No, no, no, no—"

But by then it was too late. Anna waved enthusiastically at the two young lovers. "Hi, there," she said. "Foy and Louise, right?"

"That's right," Foy said, his usual cocky confidence mixed with an air of amused curiosity.

There was an awkward pause as Anna turned her smile back to Albert. He knew he had no choice but to play along. "Uh, this is Anna," he said nervously. "She's, uh . . ."

"I'm his girlfriend," Anna finished for him.

"She's my girlfriend," Albert said, reluctantly taking the cue. "The new GF. Big-time."

"*Lot* of sexual activity with us," Anna offered.

"Y-yeah," Albert stuttered, shooting her a what-the-fuck glance. He turned his focus back to Foy and Louise, trying to roll with the cards Anna had dealt him. "Nonstop. I . . . I practically *live* inside her. So . . . y'know, if you ever want to write me a letter, you have to address it *c/o Anna's Vagina*."

Louise's expression clearly indicated she'd already had enough. She clutched Foy's arm tighter. "Sweetie, why don't we go see the freak tent," she said.

"Hey, we were just about to try the shooting gallery," Anna piped in. "Wanna join?"

"Wait, what?" Albert turned to her with an expression of mild panic. The last thing he needed was for Louise to be reminded of how useless he was with a gun.

Anna smiled at Albert. "Come on, it'll be fun," she said with enthusiasm.

Louise's gaze moved up and down Anna's body. "Y'know, I actually have that same dress," she remarked coolly.

In contrast, the tone of Anna's response was warm and genuine. "Oh, you do?"

"Yeah, I wore it to the fair two years ago. Good for you for trying to bring it back."

"Well, it just seems to me that only a complete moron would throw away a perfectly good thing." She shot Albert a sly wink that made him feel suddenly, strangely protected and looked after. She turned her attention back to Foy. "Now. how 'bout that shooting gallery, huh?"

"I'm game," said Foy. "And I say we make things interesting. A nickel a target."

"That's, uh—that's a little rich for my blood," Albert objected. "How 'bout a penny?"

"What's the matter, Albert?" Foy sneered. "Is business *ba-a-a-a-a-ad*?" He laughed at his own joke. "Very well, then, a penny it is. Good Lord, Albert, you're such a *sheep*skate."

This time, Louise laughed with him.

"Louise, get ready to *shear* me on!" A big, mustachioed guffaw.

"I really love your humor," Louise whispered sweetly to Foy.

Before Albert could drop to the ground and shrivel up like a dying insect, Anna took his arm again. "Then let's get to it, huh?" She smiled, pulling Albert toward the booth.

He whispered furiously into her ear. "What the

hell are you doing? I suck balls at the shooting gallery!"

"Relax, it'll be fine," she said, giving his hand a little squeeze.

They stepped up to the booth, where Foy paid the vendor. True to character, he tossed Albert a smirk that seemed to say, *I'll take care of this. I know money's tight for you.* The vendor handed Foy a gun. Foy reached into his pocket, took out a small tin of wax, and smoothed the tips of his moustache with preening, peacockian flair. The vendor pulled a lever, and the targets popped up. There were twelve of them, each one depicting the same caricature of a bug-eyed black slave in tattered overalls, posed as if on the run. *Jesus Christ,* Albert thought, *what the hell's wrong with rabbits or ducks?* The targets appeared and disappeared at random intervals and with aggressive speed. Foy aimed his weapon and fired six times, emptying the chamber. Six targets went down.

"Six hits!" the vendor called out. "Quite a marksman!"

The crackle of applause filled the air from the small group of spectators who had gathered close by. Foy smugly handed Albert the gun. "This should be amusing," the moustachier chuckled.

Albert took the pistol and raised it with obvious reluctance. *Why the fuck would Anna do this to me?*

He fired six times. Not a single target went down. The crowd laughed derisively as he lowered his head, trying to avoid eye contact with anybody. In his peripheral vision, standing among a cluster of townsfolk, was the twelve-year-old girl with whom he'd had the awkward dinner date.

Another girl about the same age turned and whispered to her, loudly enough for Albert to hear, "Didn't you date that guy?"

"Yeah, but it didn't go so well."

"What was the problem?"

"Eh, he was kind of a loser. Plus it just sorta felt like I was dating my dad."

"Wait, aren't you dating your dad now?"

"Yeah."

"How's that going?"

"It's going good."

Foy folded his arms and stared at Albert with triumphant arrogance. "Looks like that's six cents you owe me, sheepherder."

Albert glumly fished in his pocket for the six cents that would be meaningless to Foy but that Albert would sorely miss. He counted the pennies and held them out in his palm.

But, to his surprise, Anna intercepted the money with a quick swipe. "Hang on a second," she said, giving Foy an odd smile. "You wanna make this more interesting?"

Foy folded his arms with smug curiosity and waited for her to continue.

"If I can shoot all twelve targets on Albert's behalf, you owe him a dollar," she said. "If I can't, he owes *you* a dollar."

Albert's head whipped around to face her with alarm. He most certainly did not have a dollar to squander on such an uncertain endeavor.

"Whoa, hang on—" he began, but the crowd was already catching the fever. They began to holler with excitement. "A dollar?!" "I've never seen a dollar!" "Nobody has a dollar!" "Let us see the dollar!"

Foy, however, never shifted his gaze away from Anna. "Well, now, that *is* interesting." He smirked. "All right, then. It's a bet. Do your best . . . *ma'am*." The last word was heavily greased with derision. He handed her the pistol, and she turned back to the vendor.

"May I have a second gun, please?" she asked. The vendor hesitated briefly, then handed her a second pistol. She held one in each hand as she aimed up at the targets. "Oh, one more thing," she said. "Can that machine go any faster?"

"Well, yeah, you can play double or triple speed, but that's—"

"Fastest speed you got," she said.

He nodded reluctantly and turned a metal crank on the underside of the gallery. For the first time since the beginning of the afternoon's encounter, Foy did not look entirely sure of himself. His eyes narrowed with suspicion and just a touch of what looked to Albert like fear, though he could not be sure.

During the initial two salvos, the targets had appeared and disappeared at a rapid-fire pace. But it was downright leisurely compared to what was happening now. No sooner had the little cartoon black guys popped up than they were gone again. The whole gallery looked to be one continuous blur of motion, too fast for the human eye to register.

Anna hit every target.

The vendor looked stunned. The boisterous crowd had gone utterly silent. Anna shot Albert a secret little smile that came and went as quickly as the gallery targets, then casually set down her guns.

Albert became aware that his jaw was hanging wide open. *"Holy shit,"* he whispered to no one in particular.

"That'll be one dollar," Anna said. It was now her turn to flash a smug grin at Foy, who looked properly humiliated. He reached into his coat pocket with a scowl and removed a crisp one-dollar note. The crowd went into an uproar.

"There it is!" "Dear God, look at it!" "It's beautiful!" One father scolded his young son, "Take your hat off! That's a dollar bill!"

Clearly looking to salvage at least one finger of the upper hand, Foy turned his attention back to Albert.

"Well, well. A man who lets his girlfriend do his shooting for him. Isn't *that* a fine how-do-you-do." The crowd tittered but without enough gaiety for Foy to feel redeemed. He repeated himself with more volume. "I say, isn't *that* a fine how-do-you-do!" The crowd dutifully upped their laughter in response.

Albert glared, feeling a worm of anger gnawing at his insides, but he could not for the life of him come up with a topper. "That's not funny," was his flaccid response. "You're not funny."

Foy put an arm around Louise's slender waist. "Your ex-boyfriend doesn't seem to have a sense of humor," he said. "I can see why you dumped him."

Albert had never been timid about expressing feelings of displeasure, but he did have a relatively long fuse. Foy had lit that fuse the first day Albert saw him walk out of the moustachery locked arm in arm with Louise. The pompous bastard had stolen the one true love of Albert's life, and the fuse had been growing shorter day by day since then.

It had finally reached the powder keg.

Albert lurched forward, putting himself two inches from Foy's face. "You wanna back up that attitude, asshole?"

Unaffected by the burst of hostility, Foy's expression turned to one of gleeful disbelief. "You're kidding."

"Never been more serious in my life. Pistols. You and me."

"You wouldn't have a prayer, kiddo."

"Tomorrow. 8 A.M. sharp."

A crooked smile oozed across Foy's face. "All right. Challenge accepted."

Anna, who had been silently observing the exchange between the two men, suddenly spoke up. "Ooh, gosh, y'know, tomorrow's bad for me, and I really wanna be there. How about one week from today? That work for you, *Albert*?"

There was a pointed weight to the way she said his name that sliced a tiny notch into his tenacity. "Yeah, sure," he said.

"One week," Foy affirmed. "Come on, Louise. I'll buy you some sugared butter shavings." He planted a kiss on her lips—that was clearly more of a theatrical flaunt for Albert's benefit than an expression of affection for Louise—then took her hand and led her off into the crowd.

Albert let out an exhale that could have inflated a rubber boat.

"Oh, *fuck*," he exclaimed, throwing his head back and covering his face with his palms.

"Wow," Anna said with raised eyebrows and a hint of a smile.

"What . . . the hell . . . did I just *do*?!"

"You challenged Foy to a gunfight."

The old Albert had returned. Whatever impassioned forces had taken control of his body and mind a few moments before were now long gone.

"Oh, *Jesus,*" he said, panic creeping into his voice. "I fuckin' snapped! I didn't even know what I was saying!"

"It's interesting," said Anna. "Did you see the look on Louise's face?"

"No, what do you mean?"

"She was alert. Aroused. She was impressed."

"She was?" He sounded a shred calmer.

"Yeah, she was. You had a fire in your belly for a second there, pal. And I bet you never showed her that side of you before."

He grew flustered again. "I don't *have* that side! I honestly don't know what the fuck just happened!"

"Well, you definitely got her attention. You beat that guy in a gunfight, and I bet she thinks twice about dumping you."

"You . . . you think so?"

"Yup."

"Wait a second, no! Anna, this is insane! I can't be in a gunfight! What am I, Clinch Leatherwood here? I'll get killed—"

She whirled to face Albert with a look of intensity that he had never seen from her. "Why would you say that?"

For a moment he was at a loss for words. Her entire aura of serene self-possession had blown away in an instant, and he had no idea why. For lack of an explanation, he chose to simply answer her question. "Because he's the most vicious gunfighter in the territory. Which *I* am *not*!"

"No, you're definitely not Clinch Leatherwood." The flash of tension vanished as quickly as it had appeared, and she was all Anna once more. "And don't worry. That week I bought you is enough time for me to teach you how to shoot."

Albert suddenly realized that the biggest question of the day remained unasked. "Yeah, and that's another thing—how the hell can you shoot like that? Who the hell *are* you?"

She fixed him with a sincere gaze. "My father was a gunmaker. I've been firing guns since I could walk." It was a plausible enough explanation. But before he could inquire further, she took him by the arm and led him back toward the hitching posts. "Come on, sheepboy, we've got work to do."

The sun beat down on them with ruthless oppression as they rode toward Albert's farm.

Albert stared down at the pinkish burned skin on his arms and thought, *What a terrible thing it is to be outdoors.* If you covered yourself, you baked in the heat. If you uncovered yourself, you fried in the sun. It didn't seem to bother Anna, however.

Nothing ever seemed to bother Anna.

Albert regarded his new friend with a fresh curiosity. Who was this unflappable, nerveless woman who possessed a wisdom far beyond her years and could shoot like Wyatt Earp? He had developed a quick, comfortable bond with her over the last few days—enough to share all the private details of his fragile emotional state—but, in reality, he knew very little about her . . . and he had the distinct sense that there was more to tell than he had been privy to.

As they approached the farm, the sheep began to *baa* excitedly. As usual, they were everywhere but inside the corral. One was even sitting on the front porch as if it owned the place and was waiting for somebody to serve it a mint julep. Albert sighed and ignored the problem for the moment. As Anna had requested, he went inside the barn and fetched an armload of rusty tin cans.

She gave him a reassuring wink and arranged them equidistant from one another along the top of the fence. She handed the pistol to Albert. "Okay, go ahead."

He grimaced. "I don't know what you're expecting, but I'm—"

"I'm not expecting anything, I'm just observing. Go ahead. Don't be nervous, there's nobody watching but me."

Albert reluctantly raised the pistol and closed one eye, aiming it as best he knew how. He emptied every bullet in the chamber but did not hit a single can. Even the fence itself was undamaged.

Ten reloads and ten more attempts did not change a thing. Finally he slumped to the ground in despair. "This is never gonna work," he groaned.

"Yes, it is. Will you just trust me? It'll work, and Louise is gonna come running back to you."

Albert turned to her and stared. Never in his life had he met such an enigma. "Hey," he said, "why are you being so nice to me?"

She laughed. "What's wrong with being nice?"

"Nothing, nothing, but, I mean, you show up outta nowhere, you're this complete anomaly in my world of terribleness out here—Anna, you must have a million better things to do."

"What, I can't make a new friend? When I met you, you looked like you could use one." Her expression was almost coy. *She really is quite beautiful*, Albert observed. But he still wanted answers.

"Look, I just—I really don't know anything about you," he said.

"I promise I'm not a crazy psycho chick." She smiled.

"No, that's not what I mean."

"Can I ask you something about *you*?"

"Sure."

"Why do you love Louise?"

An interesting thing happened then. Albert suddenly realized that the past two minutes were the very first since the breakup that Louise had not been in his thoughts. But, of course, the mention of her name brought her luminous image rushing right back to the forefront of his brain: her long, flowing blond locks, her velvety-soft skin, the big blue pools on either side of her petite nose . . . pools that a man could drown in . . .

He had never been asked to quantify his love for Louise, nor had he ever thought to do so. It was something that needed no explanation. It was true love, pure and simple, and he'd always accepted it at face value with eagerness and gratitude.

Thus, it took him a moment to assemble his answer. "My God, I couldn't even count all the reasons," he said. "I feel great when I'm with her. And I feel great about *myself*. I'm *proud* when I'm with her, y'know? I mean, she's the picture of class, but she's also got this fun, playful side, and of course she's insanely gorgeous. . . ."

"Well, she's quite stunning, yes," said Anna, "but honestly—and I'm sorry to say this—I really don't see what else she's got going for her."

"Oh, you just don't know her; she's got a *lot* more to her than that," Albert said with a trace of defensiveness.

"Look, I could be dead wrong, and it's only a first impression, but my sense was that she's kinda sour and self-absorbed."

"No, not at all. Trust me, I've—"

"Yes, I know, you've known her a lot longer than I have, but keep in mind you're not exactly the most objective analyst here. And also—big news—I'm a woman. Women can read other women a hell of a lot better than men can. Like I said, I could be way off base, but it's a pretty strong vibe. And for a guy like you, with so much going for *him,* I would think—"

"Well, let's not get hysterical. I'm not sure exactly what you think I have going for me."

"See, there you go, cutting yourself down again. You act like this girl was performing a charitable act by dating you. It's really frustrating. Albert, you're sweet, you're funny, you're smart. And you've made something of yourself. You know, a lot of people out here can't say that. You're a good sheep farmer."

"Oh, please, *that's* a bunch of bullshit. I suck at

sheep. Look around you. Louise is right, I can't keep track of them at all. There was a sheep in the whore-house last week."

"Really?"

"Yeah, it wandered in there, and when I went to pick it up, somehow it had made twenty dollars."

Anna laughed loudly. It was a sweet, satisfying sound. In fact, Albert was struck by just how quenching it was to hear. *Why is that?* he wondered. Had he ever felt that way when Louise laughed at one of his jokes? And then it occurred to him: Louise had *never* laughed at his jokes. She had smiled, yes. But she'd never actually *laughed*. Albert mulled this realization. *But doesn't that make those smiles that much more meaningful? Sure, we didn't neces-sarily share the same sense of humor, but she never failed with that smile after every joke. She made the effort.* Still, Anna's laughter was welcome.

"Thanks," Albert said to her. "For saying those things about me. I guess I'm not used to much posi-tivity in my life."

She put a hand on his arm. "Look, the West sucks," she said, "but your problem isn't just the frontier. It's you. You need a little confidence boost." She tightened her grip and raised his arm, helping him aim the pistol back toward the cans. "Now try again, sheepboy," she said.

He gave her a cringing smile. "Yeah, that *sheepboy* thing isn't helping the ol' confidence."

"I like *sheepboy*."

"You're basically calling me a pussy."

"Point your gun that way, pussy."

The first five bullets missed the cans by as wide a margin as before. But on the sixth shot, one of the cans went down.

"*Yes!*" she shouted gleefully, jumping like a schoolgirl. "There ya go, pussy!"

Albert stared, legitimately astonished despite himself. "Holy shit," he exclaimed, wide-eyed. "So, all I gotta do is get Foy to let me shoot seventy-one times before *he* shoots, and I win!"

Anna laughed again. "You'll get there, I promise."

During the following days she drilled him. Hard and often. Everything from tin cans on fences to hand-drawn paper targets to airborne ceramic plates. And soon, armed with the ominous knowledge that what hung in the balance was not only the love of his life but his very life itself, Albert began to improve.

The lessons were not without their bruises, of course. He grazed his big toe on the first day. On the third day he cut his wrist on a tin can. And on the fifth day he got smashed in the face by one of the ceramic plates that Anna hurled into the air for him to shoot. Although Albert's face was bleeding profusely from the gash, a trip to Doctor Harper proved less than helpful. When the doctor tried to place a blue jay near the wound so it could peck out the blood and prevent infection, Albert and Anna politely declined treatment, opting instead for a homemade dressing.

Each day he hit more and more of the targets, until at last he was hitting more than he missed. This was a milestone, and Anna felt it was time for a little reward. She waited until the approach of sunset, then took him up to the ridge overlooking Old Stump—the "swearing place" they had visited that very first night. They leaned against a rock face and stared out at the spectacular vista of the southern Arizona landscape.

"You did great today." She smiled. "You're so much better than you were before."

"I guess," he said softly. The impending reality of the gunfight was now truly beginning to sink in. *I could be dead in a couple of days,* he thought.

Anna sensed his anxiety. "Hey, I have a surprise for you," she said, reaching into the pocket of her dress. "You've earned one of Anna Barnes's very special super secret cookies." She pulled the cookie from her pocket, took a bite, and offered it to Albert.

He stared at it as if it were a live tarantula. "Wait, is this . . . is this a weed cookie?"

"Yes, it's a weed cookie." She laughed.

"Oh, no, I . . . I don't do well with that stuff."

"That's 'cause you're too uptight. This'll help. Just have a little." She moved it toward his mouth, and he backed away.

"No. No way." He squirmed. "It's like my worst fear to OD on a recreational drug."

"Albert, it's just pot. Have a small bite. C'mon, do it for me."

She had him beat. Anna had been such a pal to him since she arrived in Old Stump that he would've felt like a loser had he declined a request from her that was phrased in such a way. But his past experiences with pot—eaten or smoked—had been less than mellow. Once, after sharing a few too many puffs with a group of peer-pressuring schoolmates, he had been certain that Jim Wegman, the blacksmith, was somehow controlling the rhythm of Albert's breathing with the clang of his hammer. Another time Albert had flown into a panic when the room began to spin, so he'd lain down on the ground, only to become terrified that remaining motionless for over ten seconds was how people became paralyzed. After a good twenty minutes of lying on his back while waving his arms and legs like an upended beetle in the hopes of staving off paralysis, he had finally started to regain his senses.

Albert took a crumb-sized nibble of the cookie.

"Oh, come on, more than that!" Anna snorted, grinning at him.

He took a deep breath and bit the cookie in earnest, noisily masticating with a sustained wince.

Anna gave his hand a squeeze. "And now we get to wait for the sunset."

An indeterminate amount of time later, Albert was leaning stiffly against the rock face, doing everything in his power to keep Anna from discovering that he was in a state of unfocused mortal terror.

"Wow, this—this is so weird. Is it supposed to be like this?" he said, trying to sound nonchalant but feeling like something had gone horribly wrong with his swallowing reflex. *Can throat muscles just shut down? Is that a thing? Like, some sort of instant throat atrophy? I won't ever be able to eat solid foods again. I'll have to pour liquefied food and water down my throat. But wait—how do I make sure it goes into my esophagus and not into my trachea? I could drown. Oh, my God, I'm gonna die by drowning! Wait, no, I could build a special funnel. Like a throat funnel. To guide the liquid food down the right tube. Edward would help me with that. I'll ask Edward. We'll make a funnel, Edward and I. With a funnel, I can live.*

Anna was too perceptive to be fooled by his casual tone. She knew he was having a private freak-out and couldn't help but laugh. "Oh, my God, Albert, will you relax and enjoy the buzz?"

"I—you gave me the right amount, right? You don't think I took too much?"

"Jesus, I'm sorry I even suggested it! I thought it'd help you mellow out."

"You don't think something went wrong, right? Like . . . I'm not gonna *stay* this way, am I?"

"You're fine, just ride it out."

"But, like, you know other people who've tried that cookie, right? I mean, not *that* cookie, but one like it? Like, a sister cookie? And they're fine, right? They're still alive?"

A prairie dog popped its head up out of the ground nearby, and Albert's panic level quadrupled. "Oh, *shit*! Anna, he knows! He knows all about this!" Albert sprinted away, leaving Anna doubled over with teary-eyed laughter.

CRACK!

The Wells Fargo stagecoach came to a skull-rattling halt.

"Oh, shit," the driver cursed. He handed the reins

to the shotgun guard and stepped down off the seat. When he surveyed the damage, he knew they were going to be here awhile.

The Sherman Creek Trail was known for being relatively mild: smooth, flat ground, no steep inclines, and a more or less straight as-the-crow-flies shot from point A to point B. Thus, it was a logical route for the Wells Fargo Bank to use in transporting its gold shipments, particularly because the terrain was relatively open almost the entire length of the trail. That meant very few places for outlaws to conveniently ambush the shipments. The only exception was the Copper Corridor, a half-mile-long stretch of the trail that wound through and around a series of large natural rock formations, effectively blocking visibility beyond thirty feet at every point along the way.

The stagecoach had broken down at the center of the corridor.

The driver furrowed his brow as he looked down at the deep rut that had caused the wheel to snap off. "John, this hole's been freshly dug," he said with deep concern on his face.

The shotgun guard knew as well as he did what that meant. "Bad news," he said softly, tightening his grip on his Winchester rifle. "Look sharp."

Although the primary purpose of the Wells Fargo stagecoach was to deliver gold to its various branches throughout the territory, it was common for the company to piggyback passenger transport during such journeys as well. Thus, a well-dressed family of three—father, mother, and seven-year-old son—waited patiently inside the coach while the two men assessed the seriousness of the breakage. After a few moments, the driver opened the carriage door and addressed the man inside. "I'm very sorry about this, sir, but we need another body."

The man sighed with mild annoyance. "It's all right." He climbed outside to assist them.

Realizing that he had a bit of time to spare, the young boy scrambled to follow his father.

"Don't you go far, Michael," his mother said.

"I won't, Mama. I'm gonna look for lizards."

The woman shuddered. "Don't you dare bring any of those awful things in here."

"I won't, Mama, I promise." He scurried out the door and ran across to the edge of the trail. It felt good to run. They'd been cooped up inside the carriage for two days straight, and a young boy couldn't burn off all his excess energy by fidgeting alone. He scanned the area with sharp eyes, eagerly anticipating the perennial boyhood thrill of capturing a live reptile. As luck would have it, he didn't have to look far. A tiny lizard darted out from beneath a rock and skittered up the trail. The boy took off in pursuit. As he raced after his quarry, the boy marveled that the lizard's tiny legs could move with enough speed and agility to make the chase an evenly matched one.

The lizard darted out of sight around one of the large monolithic rock formations that lined the edges of this part of the trail. The boy raced around the corner after it—

—and got the wind knocked out of him. He lay on his back for a moment, allowing his head to clear. When he sat up, he found himself staring at a group of four rough-faced riders, led by the coldest-looking man he had ever seen.

The boy knew something of the famous outlaws of the West from reading stories and playing games with his schoolmates, and, like any boy his age, he was fascinated by the glamorous, adventure-filled lives they seemed to lead. In the eyes of a seven-year-old, these were heroes of a sort, possessing colorful, ribald, charismatic personalities that honey-coated their dastardly acts, making them entirely forgivable.

He could tell instantly that he was looking at a real-life outlaw. However, this man was nothing like the rustlers, train robbers, and gunfighters he'd read about. There was no swashbuckling magnetism here, only a frosty darkness that emanated from eyes as reptilian as the little lizard that had surely by now made its escape. There was something about this man that struck a deep terror into the boy's heart.

The man knelt down to face the boy. "Hello there, young fella," he said with a smile bereft of kindness.

The boy sat frozen as the man leaned closer and lightly patted his knee, a sinister caricature of paternal warmth.

"What are you doing out here?"

"I'm—I was . . . I was chasing a lizard," he said, his voice quavering.

"Ah, I used to chase lizards when I was your age. You catch him?"

"N-no, he—he got away."

"Oh, that's too bad. Are you out here all alone?"

"My mom—my mommy and daddy are here."

"They are? Well, that's a comfort, isn't it? The trail's a dangerous place for a little boy to be roaming about all by himself." The man rose to his full height, his sharply hooked brows lifting slightly. "You know, I think I'd like to meet your mommy and daddy."

The three men were still struggling to pull the ruined carriage out of the rut when the shot rang out. The driver, the shotgun guard, and the well-dressed man froze and looked up at the sound. The woman, who rested uncomfortably on a nearby rock, ceased fanning herself and stared with dread at the new-comers. A group of four, all dangerous-looking, all armed. And their weapons were aimed at the three men. Her young son sat atop the lead rider's horse, stiff with fright.

Clinch aimed his gun at the head of the shotgun guard. "Drop it," he instructed calmly. With reluctance, the man slowly lowered his Winchester to the ground.

The boy's mother bolted to her feet. "Michael!" she cried out.

"Oh, you needn't worry about your boy, ma'am," Clinch said with a tip of his hat. "He's gonna be just fine . . . provided you all do as you're told." He nodded back to the burly man who flanked him on his right. "Do the honors, Ben."

Ben dismounted, strode over to the wagon, and lifted up the top of the driver's seat, where the Wells Fargo lockboxes were customarily hidden. Sure enough, he pulled out a medium-sized wooden box coated in peeling green paint. "Got it, Clinch!" he shouted excitedly. The box was sealed with a large padlock. Ben set the box down on the ground and, with just a couple of shots fired, managed to break open the lock. He lifted the lid. "Sweet Jesus, will you look at that," he uttered with a wide-eyed grin. He turned and presented it to Clinch, displaying its glittering contents.

Clinch's reptilian eyes lit up like a summer storm. "Ten thousand in pure gold bullion," he whispered with quiet intensity.

All the outlaws were transfixed by the rows of gold bars, which screamed the promise of a future gilded with creature comforts. Even young Michael, despite his terror, could not help but let a small gasp escape his lips.

There will never be another chance, the shotgun guard realized. He very slowly lowered his hand toward his boot, where he had hidden a spare derringer for just such an eventuality.

"Ten thousand, hell," said Ben. "There's gotta be at least fifteen here!"

Clinch ran a dusty finger over the bars. "We'll kindly relieve the Wells Fargo company of this heavy burden."

The guard quietly pulled the pistol from his boot. The outlaws were still focused greedily on the contents of the lockbox. The lead rider's head was bent low over the gold, which meant as clear a head shot as there would ever be without risk of killing the boy.

The guard pulled the trigger. *CRACK!*

And suddenly his gun was on the ground, as one of his fingers sailed away behind him. The barrel of the lead rider's pistol was smoking. The guard screamed in pain as he clutched his crippled hand.

"*That,*" said Clinch, "was a mistake."

Clinch dismounted, leaving the boy sitting alone atop the disproportionately large horse. He approached the stricken guard and shoved him roughly against the side of the carriage. "Listen to me closely," said Clinch with a deadly soft tone as he pressed the cold steel of his pistol against the other man's throat. "You're very lucky. Do you know that? Because I've recently come into possession of fifteen thousand dollars in gold bullion. Which means I'm in a good mood today. Now, are you gonna try that again?"

"N-no. No, sir," squeaked the petrified guard.

"You know that'd be stupid. Yes, you know that, don't you?"

"Y-yes."

"Good, good. Because I'm gonna give you just one warning: You reach for that rifle again, and *this* will happen."

Clinch fired, destroying the man's throat. The guard slumped to the ground, leaving a trail of blood smeared down the side of the carriage.

"Like I said—one warning."

The members of Clinch's gang were still busy ogling the shiny gold bars, so no one noticed until Michael was already off the horse and sprinting toward his mother's open arms. One of the outlaws turned, spotted the boy halfway, and raised his gun to shoot.

"Jordy, put your gun down!" Clinch snapped. "He's just a little boy." Clinch causally strode back over to the gang, where he promptly backhanded Jordy across the mouth. The man collapsed into the dirt, wiping his bleeding face. "Now, let's get one thing good and clear before you all start feeling too much of the gold fever," Clinch continued with a commanding tone. "Nobody's doing a goddamn thing with this haul until it cools down. We'll head back to Old Stump, pick up Lewis and Anna, and then lay low for at least a month. Understood?"

The boys grunted a chorus of affirmatives.

And so Clinch's gang rode away, leaving behind a wrecked carriage, its helpless driver, a traumatized family, and a bloody corpse.

The barn was far and away the largest in Old Stump—too large, in fact, for the farm it belonged to. Chester Cooksey had once owned vast amounts of adjacent farmland, until a particularly bad harvest season had forced him to sell off a large chunk of it in order to make ends meet. As a result, he was left with a lot of unused barn space. So, partly to help out a local citizen but mostly because it was the perfect location, the town of Old Stump tossed Chester a modest amount of compensation each year to allow the use of the barn for the annual dance. It was, Albert had noted many times, a great opportunity to once a year put on uncomfortable clothes and cram yourself into an enclosed space with all the people you see every single day.

And he and Anna were uncomfortably dressed indeed on that hot-as-hell, dry-as-fuck Friday evening as they strode through the entryway into the festively decorated barn. Colorful streamers hung from the rafters, lanterns were strewn here and there along the ceiling framework, and . . . well, that was about it. *Great job, decorating committee. Way to reach for the stars,* he thought as he shifted awkwardly in his itchy wool three-piece Sunday best. But, as miserable as he was, Anna appeared even more so. The dress she wore was the fashion of the day and looked as if it had been created by an apparel designer with an advanced brain tumor. It was hard to tell which layer was which, there were more bows than a rich kid's wrapped Christmas gift, and the bustle on the rear stuck out almost four and a half feet.

"Well, this'll be fun," she deadpanned. "It's nice to put on some loose, comfortable clothes and just relax, y'know?"

"Yeah, I love formal frontier dress," muttered Albert. "How many foot undergarments are you wearing?"

"Let's see, I've got two pairs of wool calf pantaloons, three pairs of Dutch socks, a set of bear-hide foot mittens, and a brace of wood-button overshoes. You?"

"Uh, I've got four pairs of Dutch socks, one set of sealskin ankle moccasins, two layers of Klondike heel officers, and a blanket-lined oilcloth foot coat."

"I'm really comfortable," she said, adjusting layer number 47.

"Me too. I'm glad I remembered the six items I somehow require to hold up my pants."

He turned his attention to her rear end. "I like your bustle, by the way."

"Thanks," Anna said. "Yeah, I love that the most alluring fashion statement a woman can make today is to simulate a fat ass."

"If I was a black guy, that's the meanest trick you could play on me."

"Especially 'cause, when you lift it up, it's just a big metal cage." She raised the back of her dress to reveal the bustle's support system: a complex curved iron framework that resembled a warship under construction.

"Look at that," said Albert. "You are ready to relieve the stress of the day."

"Completely."

Albert sighed and surveyed the crowded room. Despite the heat, everyone was dancing gaily, and looking as though they had no cares or concerns in the world. Albert himself was not so fortunate. His dreaded confrontation with Foy loomed roughly twelve hours away, and although he had made significant strides in his marksmanship under Anna's adept tutelage, the outcome was still far from a lock. Over the past few days, he had even begun to wonder whether the potentially mortal price of the risk offset the gain. A week ago, such a thought would not even have occurred to him. He loved Louise with all his heart, but he was noticing tiny cracks in his resolve, and he did not understand why. His stomach still corkscrewed whenever he laid eyes on her, but it was now almost like a reflex: a whack on the funny bone. It was also a bit more fleeting in duration. There were even points during the day when his mind was elsewhere. There was no question that the thought of being without her was still abhorrent, but that feeling now presented itself in a slightly more . . . *habitual* way.

He shook off his thoughts. They were irrelevant. The gunfight was tomorrow, and there was no backing out now, lest he be branded even more of a coward. And why should he want to back out anyway? Louise was worth risking his life. She was his soul mate.

Wasn't she?

"Well, this'll be a fun way to spend my last night alive," he said wryly.

"Hey," she said, "you're gonna be okay tomorrow. You've come a long way since the fair."

He wiped a sheen of sweat off his brow. "Why the hell does everything in the West always have to be settled with violence anyway? This is the '80s, for Christ's sake. Let's be civilized."

Anna turned to face him and took both his hands in hers. They were surprisingly cool against the extreme heat of the room, and they felt good. "Do you trust me?" she said.

Again he had the nagging awareness that he knew very little about this woman, but when he stared into those confident hazel eyes, he felt that somehow it didn't matter. He *could* trust her. "Yeah. I do."

Anna pushed away a strand of hair that was hanging over her left eye.

One of her eyes is a lighter hazel than the other, he observed. He had been with her every day for the past week. How had he not noticed that until now?

"Good." She smiled warmly, squeezing his hands. "If I thought you were gonna lose this gunfight, I'd make you call it off. Understand?"

He believed her. "Yeah. Okay."

She really is very—

His thoughts were interrupted by Edward's shouting. "Hey! Albert! Anna! Hi!" He and Ruth came bounding over to where they were standing.

Anna gently let go of Albert's hands.

"They're gonna start the sweethearts' dance pretty soon," Edward announced with excitement. "You guys wanna join? Oh, and how great is this band, huh?"

"Yeah, they're fantastic," Albert said drily. He cupped a hand to his mouth and shouted at the stage, "I just wanna point out that all your instruments were made for another purpose!"

The jolly group of musicians playing the washtub bass, the jug, the spoons, the comb, the saw, the dirt-shovel guitar, and the pie-plate banjo either did not hear him or chose to ignore the comment.

"Okay, let's all line up for the sweethearts' dance!" shouted the burly, red-faced master of ceremonies.

Anna did not waste any time as she grabbed Albert's arm and yanked him toward the dance floor. "Come on!" she said eagerly.

"Oh, Jesus, no, I suck at dancing."

"No one'll notice; you suck at everything." She gave him a playful wink and dragged him onto the dance floor with surprising strength.

Her enthusiasm was infectious and managed to partially cut through Albert's layers of negativity.

He felt helpless to prevent the trace of a smile that crept across his face.

The smile evaporated as he saw Foy and Louise also step onto the dance floor, dressed to the nines and holding hands.

Foy spotted Albert immediately. "Well, hello there, sheepie."

Albert stiffened. "Hello, Foy. Louise."

"Hi, Albert," Louise said flatly.

She looked beautiful in a light-blue evening dress with cream-colored lace trim. But something was missing. No matter what she wore, from frilly formal attire to everyday outdoor clothing, she always had a glow about her. That glow was absent tonight. Albert realized with a jolt that this was the first time since he'd met her that it was not present. Was something wrong with her?

"Tomorrow's a big day, isn't it?" Foy smirked cockily. "Care for a last dance?"

Albert was confused. "With you?"

"No."

"Oh, you mean—yeah, no, we're gonna dance. Anna and me."

The burly master of ceremonies spoke again. "And now to serenade us for the sweethearts' dance, our very own Marcus Thornton!"

The owner of Old Stump's livery stables stepped

into the glow of the kerosene footlights, his bushy moustache and wild hair making him instantly recognizable from afar. Marcus was well known throughout the town as a golden-voiced lothario, and the ladies in the room perked up as the band played him on with a jaunty intro.

"Ready for terrible, weird, stiff, traditional frontier dancing?" Albert said as he and Anna took their place among the other couples.

"Thank you, friends!" Marcus Thornton called out cheerily from the stage. "And now I'd like to serenade you with a lively tune by the great Stephen Foster! This is a request tonight from my friend and yours, Mr. Foy Ellison!"

Foy flashed Albert a grin that looked as though he'd rented a couple dozen extra teeth just for the occasion, as Marcus Thornton began bellowing the song in his deep, operatic baritone:

> *You men who are looking for love*
> *Don't ever give up in despair*
> *For I'll tell you a secret I know*
> *To capture the hearts of the fair*
> *Now, maybe you haven't the looks*
> *Or maybe you haven't the dash*
> *But you'll win any girl anywhere*
> *If you've only got a moustache!*

A moustache! A moustache!
If you've only got a moustache!

You may be the lowest of low
With nary a glimmer of pride
But you needn't be born of a king
To make any maiden a bride
No matter you haven't the name
No matter you haven't the cash
You can make any woman your own
If you've only got a moustache!
A moustache! A moustache!
If you've only got a moustache!

You may be as fat as a bull
You may be as ugly as sin
The ladies are shutting you out
You're wondering how to get in
Well, here is a piece of advice
For making a hell of a splash
You can turn every head at the ball
If you've only got a moustache!
A moustache! A moustache!
If you've only got a moustache!

A moustache! A moustache!
Big moustache! Thick moustache!

My moustache! Your moustache!
How I love the word moustache!
A moustache! A moustache!
If you've only got a moustache!

"God," said Albert. "I hate it here."

Anna whispered to him conspiratorially, "Hey, what do you say I steal a bottle of whiskey and we hit the road?"

Albert's shoulders slumped with relief. "I *love* that idea."

She smiled and strode briskly across the room to the bar. "Your dick's out," she said to the bartender. He glanced down with alarm, at which point she grabbed a bottle from the countertop, along with two glasses. When he looked up, both woman and bottle were gone. Anna had never even broken stride.

But rather than heading back to Albert, she stopped at an empty table in the corner of the barn. She set both glasses on the table and quickly glanced over each shoulder. When she was satisfied no one was watching, she subtly removed a paper pouch from her sleeve. She emptied its contents—a small quantity of white powder—into one of the glasses. She tossed away the paper and scanned the room. Foy and Louise were seated five tables over. Anna made her move.

"Hi," she said as she approached them. Foy

looked up, bristling visibly when he saw who it was. "Listen, Albert and I are gonna split," she continued, "but I just wanted to wish you good luck for tomorrow."

"Thank you." He smiled coldly.

"You're welcome," she countered with warmth. "So . . . I guess it's weird knowing that a woman can outshoot you, huh?"

Foy leaned back, folding his arms. "If you don't mind, my girlfriend and I are enjoying each other's company."

She plowed ahead. "But you know what the real kicker is? I can outdrink you too."

Foy relaxed a bit, and she saw his confidence bubble up again. "That, I can assure you, is impossible."

Anna flashed a mischievous smile as she held up the bottle and glasses, carefully obscuring the white powder with her hand. Without another word, she filled both glasses two thirds of the way and handed the tainted one to Foy.

She raised her glass to him. "Ten cents to the winner."

He raised his glass in response. "Agreed."

"One . . . two . . . three." They pounded the whiskey like a pair of pros. But Foy finished first, slamming his glass down onto the table, victorious. Anna swallowed her last gulp and coughed as she set her empty down next to his. She frowned at it with a perfectly simulated air of abashment. "Shit," she muttered softly, but with enough volume to reach Foy's ears.

"Don't feel bad," he said with an ugly little smirk. "Alcohol doesn't harmonize well with a woman's frail constitution."

"Guess not," she responded matter-of-factly, tossing the coins onto the table in front of him. "Here you go. You can buy your girlfriend a brain."

"Excuse me?" Louise straightened defensively.

For the first time during the exchange, Anna dropped her controlled façade. "You're an idiot. You have the nicest guy in the world throwing himself at your feet, and you're here with this complete asshole."

"Who I go out with is my own business," Louise said curtly. "So why don't you mind your own, bitch?"

Anna shook her head in wonderment. "You know," she said, "you have very lovely, very big blue eyes. No one would ever know you were blind." Anna whirled around and strode away, her bustle swaying back and forth as it vanished into the crowd.

Although nearly every member of the population of Old Stump had gathered to participate in the dance that night, the one individual who was forced to abstain, thanks to the very nature of his profession, was Sheriff Arness. He stood sullenly at the potbelly stove across from his desk, slowly stirring a watery stew of beef and vegetables for his dinner. His wife had been trampled by cattle three years ago, and since then Millie the brothel madam had gotten into the habit of bringing him his meals as a sort of unofficial courtesy. Whether it was out of pity for his loss, or whether she had romantic designs of her own, no one knew—not even the sheriff—but he was nonetheless grateful for the kindness.

Tonight, however, Millie was whooping it up at the barn dance along with the rest of the town, so it fell to Sheriff Arness to cook his own dinner. To make the task even more disagreeable, he had to prepare enough for his prisoner. *Seems downright stupid to waste good beef on a dead man,* he thought bitterly. Lewis Barnes was being held for shooting the pastor's son until a U.S. marshal could be dispatched to Old Stump to take him into custody. Lewis would get a trial, of course, but because of Pastor Wilson's blood connection to a congressman, that trial would be primarily for show. Lewis Barnes would be executed before the month was out.

The sheriff ladled three spoonfuls of stew onto

his own plate and then a single spoonful on a plate for Lewis. He spat a mucus-filled glob of saliva on top for good measure, then retrieved the cell key from his desk. Lewis was fast asleep on his cot against the far wall. Plate in hand, the sheriff cautiously unlocked the cell door. As soon as it was open, he pulled his gun out of its holster and aimed it at the slumbering prisoner. "Suppertime, you lazy prick," he growled.

Lewis remained unconscious, his soft, rhythmic snores echoing off the walls of the sparse cell.

The sheriff slowly set the plate down on the floor. He straightened up again and stared at the sleeping man with distaste. "Goddamn waste of lungs." He turned back toward the cell door—

—and was out cold before he even felt the blow.

It was as mild a night as the desert ever deigned to offer its human tenants, and the stars were out in theatrical plenitude. Albert and Anna sat on the uneven fence next to Albert's farmhouse and swapped jolting pulls from the whiskey bottle.

Albert took a swallow and winced as the burning amber liquid blazed a trail from his throat down to his stomach. He shook off the intensity of the taste with a high-frequency shiver and turned to Anna. "I have that goddamn moustache song stuck in my head," he complained.

"Just think of another song," she suggested.

"I can't; there's only like three songs."

"That's true, and they're all by Stephen Foster."

"Ugh, yeah." Albert grimaced.

"You don't like his music?"

"I dunno, I'm . . . on the fence about it."

Anna rolled her eyes at his pun. "Wow, now I hope you get shot tomorrow."

Albert laughed and looked at her fondly. "Listen," he said with sincerity, "whatever happens tomorrow . . . I just wanna say thank you. And y'know, this may be the booze, or your pep talk earlier, or both, but . . . I think I can do it. I can beat him."

Anna gave his arm a squeeze as she took another swig of whiskey. "Like I said, you'll be fine. And in case you haven't noticed, you sound a lot more confident than that guy who pulled me out of the saloon not too long ago."

Albert thought back to that night. It seemed like a year ago. In reality, it had been . . . what, two weeks? Not even. He felt as though he'd known Anna Barnes so much longer. He could trust her. And yet, paradoxically . . .

"Anna, I have to ask you something. I feel as close to you as any friend I've ever had. Which is fucked up, because the glaring fact is, I still don't really know *anything* about you. And every time I ask, you change the subject."

Anna sighed and lowered her head. Usually, her acute mind would quickly arm her with a sharp, confident response to any question, but this time she did not speak.

Albert got the distinct sense that he was about to get the real story. In a way, he did.

"I know it seems like I've been secretive with you," she said, "and . . . look, to be honest, here's how it is: I don't much like where I come from. I don't like it at all. It's a rotten place, and as far as I'm concerned, I'd just as soon erase it from my life. And it's not who I am today. I know it's asking a lot, but . . . don't ask me about it. Okay?"

Albert's curiosity was now twice as piqued; he desperately wanted to pry deeper. Instead, he offered his best sympathetic smile. "Okay."

"Thanks," she said with visible relief. The playfulness immediately returned to her tone. "Now, how 'bout a toast to something we both have in common: our hatred of this terrible part of the country." She raised the whiskey bottle. "Fuck the West!" She took a sizable pull and passed it to Albert.

"Fuck the West!" he echoed, and tossed back a swig of his own.

There were only a couple more shots left in the bottle. "If you want to kill it, go ahead," she offered.

"No, I can't," he said. "I've had enough already, and when I drink too much, it doesn't shit well."

"Doesn't *sit* well." She laughed, raising the bottle to her lips.

"No, *shit*. It causes horrible shits. The morning after I drink too much, when I sit down to go to the bathroom, it feels like a madman trying to punch his way out of my asshole."

Anna laughed so hard, the whiskey came squirting out of her nostrils.

"See, that's what happens, right there," Albert said, laughing along with her. "I need at least half the Old Testament in the john with me, that's how long it takes. Ironically, it usually settles down by the time I get to the part in Leviticus where it says, *No butt stuff*."

"Okay, stop! You're gonna make me drown!" She coughed, shoving him coltishly.

Albert straightened. "Ooh, I almost forgot," he said with excitement. He called toward the corral. "Bridget! Come here, Bridget! *Baaaa! Baaaa!*"

Bridget emerged from the flock of sheep and hurried over toward the fence, bleating back at Albert. She had something strapped to her back, Anna noticed. As Bridget came to a stop next to the fence, Anna saw that it was a wooden tray with a small wrapped gift sitting on top.

"What's this?" she asked with amusement.

"Ah, it's not much. Just a little something to say thanks."

She looked at Albert with suspicious but affectionate eyes and carefully unwrapped the paper. Inside, she found a picture frame with a photograph in it. It was a young, scruffy-looking cowboy leaning against a barn—

—with a big grin on his face.

Her eyes snapped wide open. *"Holy shit!!"*

"I know, right?!" Albert said giddily.

"He's *smiling*! In the *picture*!"

"I know! I bought it off a peddler who was coming through town a few days ago."

"This is the guy I heard about! I can't even believe this exists!"

"Yeah, and apparently he's not insane."

"Bullshit."

"That's what the guy told me."

"It takes thirty seconds to take a photograph. He would've had to smile for thirty sustained seconds."

"I know. I've never been happy for thirty seconds in a row in my life."

"It's the West—no one has. He's gotta be insane."

"Yeah, probably."

She turned to him with a look of enormous gratitude. "Albert, this was really kind of you."

"Oh, please, I owe you. A lot more than this, actually."

She kissed him on the cheek. Her touch was warm, and her scent was a fragrant sweetness that stood in glaring incongruity with the malodorous stink of the surrounding frontier.

Albert kissed her.

She did not pull away. For several moments, they both allowed the world around them to melt into nonexistence.

When the kiss ended, Albert was acutely aware that his cheeks were bright red. He felt stimulated, alive, and supremely confused. He opened his mouth to speak, with no clue as to what was going to come out. "Oh," he said.

She looked at him with seemingly new eyes. "What?" she said softly.

"I'm . . . I'm sorry. I shouldn't have done that."

"It's okay."

"I—you've just . . . you've been a good friend to me, that's all."

"It's really okay," she said, putting a gentle hand on his.

"Plus, I've had a shitload of whiskey."

She laughed. "Me too. I know, it's fine. I should probably go anyway."

Albert looked down self-consciously at his shoes. "I'll take you home."

The desert night had chilled somewhat as they walked side by side up to the door of the Old Stump Hotel. They paused in the entryway.

"Good luck tomorrow," she said with warm reassurance. "I'll be there."

"Thanks," he said. They stood there under the lamplight for what seemed like an eternity, and then she kissed him back.

Where their first encounter had been sweet, gentle, and delicate, this one was passionate. He returned it in kind. *What the hell am I doing?* he thought. *I'm about to risk my life to win back the woman I love. I love Louise.*

But he stayed.

For several minutes they allowed the moment to take its own shape as they held each other, relishing the shared body heat that warmed them in the brisk air.

Then at last Albert stepped back and released his hands from hers. He could feel his smile touching his eyes, something he had not felt in a conspicuously long time. "Good night," he said, and turned to walk away. He strode off toward the hitching post as Anna closed the hotel door behind her.

Neither of them noticed the murky figure of Lewis watching from the shadows of the alley across the street.

"You can't call it off?" Louise asked Foy, making a swirling motion against his bare chest with her pale, petite finger.

"Of course not!" he said sharply. "I'd be branded a coward."

"But, baby, if you fight him tomorrow, you're gonna kill him."

"Yes, that's what happens in a gunfight," he said with condescension.

They lay side by side in Foy's generously proportioned brass bed. His home was easily the most well appointed in Old Stump and the only house that contained any polished wood.

"Look, he's not a bad guy, Foy. I mean, yeah, he's kind of a loser and he always smells like sheep, but he doesn't deserve to be shot."

"Louise, my decision is final. Now do it."

She pouted. "But I'm tired."

"*Louise*," he said sternly. She sighed, leaned in toward his face, and began to dutifully suck on one tip of his moustache.

He closed his eyes as he shifted his body in arousal. "Mmm . . ." he moaned, his brow moist and his lips parted. "My social stature is significant. I'm an important man. I have my own business. People envy me." Then suddenly his eyes snapped open. He sat up rigidly, leapt out of bed, and dashed out of the room.

"Foy?" Louise called after him. "What's wrong? Foy?"

She heard him race out the front door. She opened the window and looked out. It was dark, but she could make out his bare-assed naked form sprinting across the yard to the outhouse. He slammed the wooden door with the crescent moon carved in its surface and swore loudly as explosive diarrhea claimed him for the next half hour.

The morning of the gunfight was bright and clear, the air mild. Anna brushed her hair in preparation as she stared at herself in the hotel room's full-length mirror. She had more on her mind than she cared to contend with, as she had not expected events to play out the way they had. Albert had been a project: a fun sort of diversion while she bided her time in the sleepy town of Old Stump, pending the inevitable return of Clinch. Albert had been a toy, one she'd become extremely fond of. But now things had changed. *She* had changed.

Anna wasn't worried about the gunfight. Albert

would be fine. He would never be a crack shot, of course, but he wouldn't need to be. Foy would be too sick to hold a gun, let alone shoot straight, assuming he showed up at all. But she *was* worried about herself. What had happened could not be undone. And yet how could it be faced, given what her life was?

Her thoughts were interrupted by a knock at the door. She set her hairbrush down on the side table and went to answer it. It was probably Albert, wanting a last-minute pep talk before he went out to confront his opponent. But when she opened the door, the eyes that greeted her were cold and reptilian.

"Hi, sweetheart," said Clinch.

Albert stood at one end of the thoroughfare, overcome by déjà vu. This was precisely where he'd stood not so long ago as he prepared to face off against Charlie Blanche. The crowd lined both edges of the thoroughfare, just as they had for every gunfight since Old Stump's birth. Edward and Ruth gave Albert supportive looks as they watched from one side of the street, squeezing each other's hands. And there, looking on from the rows of assembled townsfolk, in almost the exact same spot she'd occupied on the day of the Charlie Blanche encounter, was Louise. On that day she'd been part of his life—an extension of himself that he'd considered as constant as the seasons, as vital as a limb.

And now? She was somebody else's constant. But as much as that hurt, it was a very different strain of hurt than it had been before. It cut deep, to be sure, but the pain was dull, the wound scabbing.

With Charlie Blanche, Albert had faced an opponent who was sharp, tough, and ready for action. However, the man who stumbled into position at the other end of the street today looked ready for nothing short of the grave. The crowd murmured with uncertainty as Foy shuffled out into the street, looking sweaty and sunken-eyed. Nonetheless, he managed to muster up a passably cocky grin. "Well, now. I didn't think you'd show, sheepie."

Albert sized him up as he tried to determine exactly what was happening with the man. It didn't matter, he supposed. "Um, yeah," he said. "Listen, Foy, you—"

Albert was cut short by a sharp hand gesture with clear meaning: *Dear God, hold on a second*. Foy clutched his stomach in obvious pain and staggered over to the edge of the street, grasping the top of a hitching post to steady himself. Suddenly his eyes widened as a look of panic crossed his face. One arm reached out feebly for a black bowler hat sitting atop the head of a very surprised-looking bearded

man observing from the street's periphery. Foy
snatched the hat off the man's head, threw it on the
ground with the inside facing upward, yanked down
his trousers, and squatted on top of it. A blast of
diarrhea issued forth with the pressure of a burst
steam engine, completely filling the hat. Foy
straightened and started to pull up his trousers in a
pitiful attempt to salvage some measure of dignity.
But before he could get the trousers to his waistline,
a second wave overtook him. He turned to the opposite side of the thoroughfare and reached flac-
cidly for another man's hat. The second man
flinched and backed away, having no desire to submit his hat to the fate that would surely befall it
should he relinquish possession. Foy persisted,
matching the man's retreat with weak, stumbling
advances. With a final burst of energy, Foy's arm
struck out and seized the hat, throwing it to the
ground as before. He unloaded a second shipment
of watery shit.

Albert watched uncomfortably as Foy stood up,
winded and wheezing. Foy refastened his trousers
(Albert did not want to think about the conspicu-
ous absence of post-evacuant hygiene) and took his
position once again.

"All . . . all done?" asked Albert.

"I'm ready," Foy croaked, looking far from done.

Albert nodded, put both hands on his gun belt . . .

. . . and unclasped it, letting his gun fall to the ground.

Foy stared at him, utterly baffled despite his condition. The crowd murmured with confusion.

"Foy," said Albert, a tone of uncharacteristic confidence in his voice, "she's all yours."

The crowd's murmuring rose as they struggled to assimilate this unusual development. They didn't have to wait long for an explanation, as Albert turned to face the woman who had driven him to this place on this day.

"Louise," he said, "you are . . . God, you are so beautiful. And I really do care about you. But . . . I don't know—I think somewhere along the line I forgot that a relationship is a two-way street. And I've been reminded recently of what it's like to have someone care about *me*. And you know what? I like it. So if you wanna spend the rest of your life with a pussy full of hair, I say go with God and best of luck to you."

Albert gave her a gentlemanly tip of the hat and strode away from the thoroughfare with a lightness and an optimism that he had not felt in a very long time. After a moment, however, he turned around to face the crowd again.

"I just realized, that joke may not have been clear.

I didn't mean that she has a hairy pussy; I meant that Foy has a moustache, so . . . she gets hair in her . . . when he . . . goes down there. Yeah." He smiled gamely and walked away once more.

One cowboy in the crowd spoke up. "*I* got it."

Albert practically sprinted up the steps of the hotel. *Maybe Anna was watching from her room,* he thought, knowing full well that was absurd. She should have been there to support him. Regardless, whatever her reason for being absent, he knew he would forgive her. He felt too good today. Too intoxicated with liberation.

In fact, he realized that he had become accustomed to waking up every morning feeling like shit. There was a normalcy to it that had taken up residence in his body and soul. As he took the stairs two at a time, he thought, *I feel great. Is this what I've been missing out on? How could I have spent so much of my life being denied this feeling?*

He reached Anna's room at the top of the stairs and banged excitedly on the door.

"Anna!"

There was no answer.

Albert knocked again and then tried the knob. It was unlocked, and he poked his head inside and

looked around. The bed was unmade. A full wash-
basin sat on the side table. A hairbrush lay on the
floor. But the room was empty.

"Hey, guys, have you seen Anna?" Albert asked as
he puffed up the street toward Ruth and Edward.
The rest of the crowd had more or less dispersed,
grumbling to themselves with dissatisfaction over
the lack of bloodshed.

"No," said Ruth. "Not since last night at the
dance."

"Huh," he said, at a complete loss.

"Albert . . . it's her, isn't it?"

Albert smiled. "Yeah. It's her."

"You love her."

"Yeah. I do. And what's even better is, I think she
might love me back."

Edward grinned. "Oh, that is so great. I think
she's so neat."

"So nobody's seen her, huh?" Albert was now
beginning to worry. "I don't understand. She said
she'd be there this morning. She wouldn't just not
show up."

Ruth patted his arm. "I'm sure she's fine, Albert.
And she'll turn up soon. Especially if what you said
is true."

"Yeah, I guess so. . . ."

"Hey, in the meantime, why don't we all get outta this heat and go have a beer, huh?" Edward suggested.

They made their way into the saloon, ordered three glasses of beer, and sat down at their usual corner table.

"Hey, um, Albert?" said Edward with an awkward expression on his face.

"Yeah?"

"Do you think you and Anna will have sex?"

Albert was caught off guard. "I . . . I dunno. I mean . . . maybe at some point."

"Well, when you do, how about let's make it like an all-us-friends thing. Like, we all get, like, in sync. Sexually."

"Eddie, we're not having sex," Ruth said flatly.

Edward hung his head in shame. "I'm sorry, I know, it was a stupid idea."

"Ruth! Let's fuck!" shouted the dirty cowboy from the stairwell.

"Coming!" She hurried off to do her job.

"She keeps my head on straight," said Edward gratefully.

Albert was about to question that, when they heard the sound of approaching hooves outside. The saloon was fairly packed with townsfolk who had dragged their asses all the way from home to watch a gunfight that hadn't occurred, and they'd now turned their attention to drinking and gambling, for lack of anything better to do. They all looked up as two perspiring local farmers hurried into the saloon, wearing expressions of abject terror.

The hoofbeats came to a halt just outside. Albert and Edward heard the sound of spur-heeled boots ascending the wooden steps. The batwing doors opened . . .

. . . and in stepped the biggest, most sinister-looking man Albert had ever seen. He was cold-eyed, dead-faced, and all too recognizable from the posters in the sheriff's office.

"Clinch Leatherwood," Edward said with horror, almost too softly to be heard.

Albert rolled his eyes in dismay. "Great. Another thing that can kill us. We should all just wear coffins as clothes."

Clinch Leatherwood brought with him a dark, bloody history, even prior to his emergence as a notoriously deadly threat to peace, law, and order on the frontier. He was born in South Carolina in 1836, the son of a poorly compensated overseer on a struggling rice plantation. His mother had died the day she gave birth to him—not as a result of the birth itself, but because a heavy summer rain had caused the roof to collapse immediately following the delivery, crushing her beyond recognition. Miraculously (or not, depending on one's point of view), Clinch had survived. His relationship with his father had, by adolescence, decayed to the ugly degree that outbreaks of physical violence between father and son were not uncommon. Inevitably, it escalated to such intensity that one night, after a particularly heated argument about which of them disliked Mexicans more, Clinch broke a whiskey bottle in half and stabbed his father in the throat with the sharp end. Having no intention of being tried for murder, the younger Leatherwood fled the scene and roamed aimlessly throughout the South for several years, successfully avoiding blame for the patricide.

Then, as luck would have it, the outbreak of the Civil War provided him with an appropriate conductor for his electric temper. Clinch enlisted in the Confederate Army, where he wound up as part of a regiment stationed in northern Virginia, not far from Union lines. However, long stretches of inaction coupled with a shortage of supplies soon brought his barely controlled rage bubbling back to the surface. A quarrel erupted one night between Clinch and a fellow noncommissioned officer over a chunk of ham. The ham had been sent to the noncom as part of a care package from his family. Clinch wanted the ham for himself, but rather than ask the noncom if he would be willing to share it,

Clinch attacked the man in his tent and beat him to death, using the ham as a blunt instrument. This time, however, there was no escaping awareness of his crime. It was a small camp, and there were witnesses who would testify to seeing Clinch emerging from the tent holding the bloody ham. Once again, Clinch fled. He made his way west, west, and farther west, until he reached the southern Arizona territory. Here, there was barely any law at all. Here, the toughest men forged the moral compass with their whims. This was where he belonged. And he had flourished, cutting a swath of terror and death through the region, creating a name for himself that struck fear into the hearts of everyone who heard it.

Clinch scanned the saloon. He took a few steps into the room. Three other rough-looking men followed, flanking him on either side. All were armed to the teeth, with two pistols apiece and fully loaded gun belts.

Everyone held their breath. Then finally, after several seconds of silent scrutiny, Clinch spoke in a low, deadly tone.

"Someone in this little shit-box town is gonna die. One of my boys saw a man kissing my wife last night. I want to know who it was."

Edward whistled softly. "Jesus."

Albert nodded. "Yeah, no shit. Someone's gonna get fuuuucked uuuuup."

Clinch offered the room a hideous, wraithlike approximation of a human smile. "You seem like good people," he said. "And good people know better than to take what isn't theirs. And this—this is mine."

He reached out through the batwing doors and, with a hard yank, pulled a woman roughly inside by the elbow. Her head was down as she tried to avoid eye contact, but even before Clinch gripped her chin and thrust her face upward, Albert knew who the woman was. His heart stopped. It was Anna.

"Oh, my God . . ."

Edward and Ruth both turned to him in shock. Albert felt as though he were watching events play out from afar. He had known all along that Anna was protecting a secret of some kind, but he'd never fathomed it could possibly be something this dark. *She's married. To Clinch Leatherwood. The deadliest, most ruthless, most murderous outlaw in all the West.*

"Now, I'm gonna ask again," Clinch said quietly. His smile had vanished. "Who is it?"

No one answered. The move happened with blinding speed, and Clinch's gun was suddenly in his hand. He pointed it at the head of one of the gamblers.

"Who?" he said.

The sound of pressurized liquid impacting fabric

could be heard as the card-playing cowboy pissed himself in fear. "I . . . I dunno," he managed to croak.

Clinch shot him in the head. The man slumped to the floor, blood slowly pooling outward from his ruined skull.

Clinch looked around at the terrified saloon patrons. "I'd very much like to be introduced to the man I'm looking for. So you all make sure he gets this message: Either he meets me in the thoroughfare at noon tomorrow—or I start killing more people."

He turned to depart, pulling Anna forcefully along with him. With great shame in her eyes, she stole a furtive glance at Albert that lasted all of a half second before she was dragged away.

The room breathed a sigh of relief. Edward and Ruth stared at their friend.

"Albert, you gotta get outta here!" urged Edward with alarm.

How fleeting Albert's dalliance with blissful clarity had been. He was devastated all over again.

The horses came to a halt in the middle of the prairie just north of Old Stump. Clinch dismounted and gave Anna a brutish yank, pulling her down from the saddle with him. Plugger moved anxiously nearby, whimpering as if he knew there was trouble afoot. Clinch thrust Anna against the side of a rock formation jutting up from the ground and made it clear with one sharp, deadly glance that any attempt to escape would be met with unchecked violence. He turned to Lewis. "There's an abandoned sod house over around that bend. We'll stash the gold there. Take the boys and set up camp. I need some alone time with my wife."

Lewis flashed Anna a rat-faced smile of vindictive satisfaction. "Will do, Clinch. C'mon, boys!"

The rest of the gang galloped away with him as Clinch turned his full attention toward his immediate concern. He approached Anna, who looked at him with the revulsion most people would have reserved for a decaying corpse. He gently caressed her cheek with one hand, then swiftly backhanded her across the face, knocking her to the ground.

"Who is it, you whore?" he growled.

She pulled herself to her feet, never taking her eyes off him. "Mark Twain," she said.

Clinch stared at her for a long moment before he finally spoke. "It is?"

"No! Jesus, how fucking stupid *are* you?"

His face twisted into a snarl, his eyes narrowing to razor-thin black slits. He drew his gun and pressed it into the center of her forehead. She pulled back slightly from the pressure but did not flinch.

"Who?" he said in his deadly soft tone.

Anna waited just long enough to make the theatrics of the moment seem convincing, then averted her gaze to the ground with an expression of shamed resignation. "It's Sheriff Arness," she said at last, turning to Clinch with moistened eyes. "Please don't hurt him, I'm begging you!" Part of her felt a pang of guilt for passing such a mortal buck to the sheriff, but he *was* the sheriff, after all. It was his job to deal with assholes like this.

Clinch made it a moot point, however. "After all these beautiful years together, you don't think I know when you're lying?" He cocked his pistol. Anna shut her eyes and prepared for the inevitable. Then, suddenly, the piercing sound of Plugger's barking split the air as the nappy mutt bounded up, growling and baring his teeth at Clinch. The outlaw looked down, and that bloodless gash of a smile split his face open.

Anna felt the barrel of the gun pull away from her forehead, and she exhaled as she opened her eyes. Her relief quickly evaporated, however, as she saw that Clinch had aimed the gun at Plugger. "Either you tell me his name," he said, "or ol' Plugger here gets a plug in his head."

She knew her options were exhausted. This time when she averted her gaze to the ground, there were no theatrics at play.

"Albert," she whispered. "Albert Stark."

Clinch lowered his gun. "There. That's much better."

For one horrifying instant Anna thought he was going to shoot Plugger anyway, but Clinch holstered his pistol.

He turned and strode back to his horse, removing his hat. "I've missed you, darling," he said. without warmth or affection. "I've missed you a lot." He removed his vest and his shirt and draped them over the saddle. His back was to her.

I'll never get another chance, she realized.

Clinch went on, while undoing his trousers, "But now we got time. We got time to be husband and wife. The proper way." His pants were only halfway down when the blow struck the back of his head. He fell to the ground, unconscious, as Anna stood over him holding the bloodied rock. His bare ass stared up at her in a most undignified way.

Anna went to mount his horse, then paused as she looked down at him again. "Ah, shit," she said. "I can't leave him like this."

She approached the base of the stone formation, picked a small flower, and stuck it in Clinch's ass crack with the bloom facing upward. "That's better," she said. She mounted his horse and raced back toward Old Stump.

Edward was one of many local businessmen nailing signs to the front doors of their establishments reading CLOSED UNTIL FURTHER NOTICE. No one was taking any chances with the gang of outlaws in town.

Ruth approached him as he was pounding away at the final nail. "Eddie?" she said, her tone indicating a subject of importance.

"Yeah, sweetheart?"

"Eddie, I've been thinking. With Clinch Leatherwood in town, and with everyone so scared, I . . . it's got me wondering."

"What is it?" he said, giving her his full attention.

"Well, any of us could die tomorrow. I mean, we don't know what's gonna happen. And . . . I think we should have sex."

His full attention doubled. "What?"

"I think we should have sex tonight."

"Okay."

"Yeah?"

"Yeah. Let's."

"I mean, under the circumstances, God will forgive us," she said, looking to him for affirmation.

He gave it to her. "I think so. We'll make sure there's a Bible in the room so God can watch. Then He can be a part of it. Ahhh, I'm getting excited now!"

Albert was hastily packing his bag when he heard the hoofbeats. His breath stopped as he hurried to the window, expecting to see Clinch and his gang descending on the farm. But when he peered out through the uneven ripples in the glass, he saw Anna galloping toward the cabin. He couldn't decide whether that was better or worse. He did not want to see her, now or ever again.

Albert went back to packing. He heard her knock on the door, but he did not respond.

"Albert!" she called out, uncharacteristic alarm in her normally rock-steady voice. "Albert, are you in there?" When he still didn't answer, she let herself in. "Albert! You've gotta get out of here!" she exclaimed.

He did not look up to make eye contact with her. "Yeah, that's exactly what I'm doing."

"No I mean, you have to leave now! Clinch is gonna be looking for you!"

Albert continued stuffing clothing, books, and cans of food into the bag. "Yeah, I'm leaving. I'm going to San Francisco. Which is what I should have done weeks ago."

She looked at him mournfully. "I'm sorry."

"Yeah, well, so am I."

Anna floundered a bit as she searched for something to say next. "What about your dad?"

"I asked him if he wanted to come, and he said no. He's up on the hill burying himself next to Mom."

She waited a beat, then spoke again. "Look . . . I never meant to mislead y—"

"Oh, Anna, don't even waste my time with that," he shot back, whirling to face her directly. "You had a million opportunities to tell me. And you fucking lied."

"I didn't lie," she insisted with a pleading tone. "I just made the choice to keep certain things to myself. I honestly, truly thought it was for the best. I would never lie to you."

Albert was privately insulted by her attempt to sell such a Jesuitical interpretation of the word. A lie of omission remained a lie. Nonetheless, he chose not to engage. "I don't care," he said flatly, and went back to his packing.

"Look, I couldn't tell you. It was for your own safety."

"Oh, bullshit."

"That, and . . . I liked you. A lot," she said with undeniable sincerity. "I didn't want to scare you away. I . . . never thought I'd meet someone like you."

"Oh, what, someone who hasn't *killed people*? Yeah, I guess that's pretty hard to find. That's why women are always saying, 'Ugh, why are all the non-murderers taken?' "

"It's not my fault, okay? We were married when I was nine!"

Albert lowered his wall just enough to release a momentary burst of genuine astonishment. "*What? Nine?* Jesus Christ, how does that even *happen*? Was there a ceremony?"

"Yeah, my parents were there, a couple of neighbors. I didn't wanna wind up one of those fifteen-year-old spinsters."

"Well, you know . . . I shouldn't be surprised," he said, more to himself than to her. "Every girl I fall in love with ends up disappointing me." He finished his packing and closed the bag.

"You . . . you love me?"

"Don't worry, I'm over it. You can go now."

For the first time since Albert had met her, Anna lost her shit. "*All right! Yes, I lied! Fine!* What should I have said? *Oh hi, I'm Anna—I've been fucking a killer since I was ten!*"

"Oh, he waited a year. What a gentleman."

"Well, late nine, I rounded up. Look, I'm done with him! I knocked him out and stuck a daisy in his asshole."

"What?"

"That's how much you mean to me."

Albert slung his bag over his shoulder. He was tired. Tired of the conversation, and tired of inviting pain into his life. "You know what? I loved a girl who doesn't even exist. I loved Anna Barnes, not Anna Leatherwood. Hell, is your name even Anna? Or is it something terrible like Gwendolyn?"

"No. It's Anna. I'm the girl you loved. That was the real me—possibly for the first time in my life. I suppose, when I really think about it, you're the first person I *haven't* lied to. Look, I never thought I deserved a good guy. But I do. I love you. Just give me one more chance. Please. We can get out of here—we'll go to San Francisco together. Start a life. All I want is to be with you."

Albert said nothing as he looked into her eyes, searching for some clue to whether she could be trusted. She was as beautiful as ever, and he wanted very much to say yes, to run off with her that very instant. But he remembered the pain of losing Louise. He'd trusted a woman with his heart, and she had betrayed that trust when he was at his most exposed. He never wanted to feel that kind of raw, numbing misery again. And if that meant never again opening his heart to love, well, then, that was a price he was willing to pay. He deflected her hazel-eyed gaze back at her with a hardened look of his own. "Sorry," he said. "I'm not gonna get fucked over again."

Before she could respond, however, the sheep began to bleat loudly from the corral. Albert went to the window and looked out. He couldn't see anything at first, but when he squinted he could make out a dust cloud in the distance, indicating the approach of a group of horses. "Someone's coming," he said.

"It's Clinch." Anna knew.

They both knew. And this time there would surely be no talk. He would kill them on sight.

Albert grabbed her by the arm and pulled her toward the door. "Go on, get out of here. There's a trail out back that leads to the ridge. Go."

"What are you gonna do? Albert, he'll kill you!"

"Don't worry about me, just go! Now!" He pushed her roughly but not unkindly through the doorway and out into the yard. She quickly mounted her horse, then hesitated, staring back at him. They shared a momentary glance, both realizing that this could be the last time they would ever see each other. Anna kicked her horse, spurring him into an immediate hard gallop. And then she was gone.

Clinch and his men roared like thunder onto Albert's farm. The already disorganized sheep flock scattered even more as they fled the onslaught of outlaw hooves. The men dismounted and burst into the cabin, ransacking everything in sight as they searched for their quarry.

After several fruitless moments, Lewis turned to his boss. "He's not here, Clinch."

They were about to look elsewhere when Clinch noticed something. A bag resting in the corner. He picked it up and opened it. It was fully packed with clothing and food. His bloodless smile made its latest appearance as he slowly drew his gun.

Albert crouched low on all fours, hoping for all the world that he wasn't visible. In each hand, he clutched a fistful of white wool, courtesy of the two sheep on either side of him. He pulled hard, making sure they didn't drift. The flock was made up of approximately sixty sheep, and Albert had concealed himself smack in the center. He knew that as long as the sheep remained grouped together, he should be able to wait out Clinch's search without being discovered.

They would turn the house upside down, find it empty, and deduce that Albert had fled. After that they would probably head back to town and scour every nook and cranny there too. By the time they realized that he had escaped, he would have such a lead that, even if they guessed which direction he'd gone, they'd never catch up.

He listened intently until finally he detected the outlaws emerging from the cabin. He waited for the sound of horses being mounted. Surely Clinch would give up the search now. But what Albert heard next reined his heartbeat to a screeching halt.

"I know you're here, Stark."

Albert noted the sinister pleasure in Clinch's voice. It chilled him to the bone. He heard the men slowly, methodically walking the premises as they searched for him. *How the fuck did he know?* And then he realized the idiocy of his mistake. *The bag.* Clinch had found the bag, opened it up, and seen the supplies. Since only a fool would leave food, water, and supplies behind when riding off into the desert, Clinch would recognize that Albert must still be here.

Albert began to panic. All that stood between him and certain death was a flock of sheep. And Clinch Leatherwood was not the type of man to leave a stone unturned. Albert would be found. And then he would be killed. There would be no explaining the situation, no pleas for mercy. He would die.

He could hear the soft jingle of multiple spurs. *They're getting closer.* He realized if he had any hope of saving his own life, he had to act soon. And then a possibility occurred to him. *Curtis. Curtis is tied to the corral fence.* It couldn't be more than fifty feet from where Albert was hidden. If he could somehow reach Curtis, he might be able to mount the horse quickly enough to get a head start. Outrunning the outlaws from that point was another matter—Albert was hardly the world's greatest equestrian—but his only alternative was to wait here and be shot.

From the recesses of his memory, Albert recalled the story of Odysseus's escape from the cave of Polyphemus. The blind Cyclops had let his sheep out to graze, feeling their backs one by one to ensure that his prisoners were not escaping. However, Odysseus and his men had cleverly attached themselves to the undersides of the giant sheep, using them to slip away to freedom, undetected. It should have been an inspiring image. But Albert was no Odysseus. And Clinch was not blind.

Albert crawled on his stomach through the packed flock, resisting the urge to retch when he felt his hands press into the soft, wet piles of sheep shit and the puddles of foul ovine urine. He slowly made his way, inch by inch, toward Curtis. How much farther did he have to go now? Thirty feet? Twenty? He would have to risk a peek. He held his breath and peered over the top of a sheep back. Curtis was now only about fifteen feet away. Depending on where the outlaws were, he might be able to sprint for it. He turned and looked in the other direction . . .

. . . and almost had a stroke. Lewis was standing within spitting distance, facing away from Albert. Albert dropped to the ground and lay motionless on his back. He dared not make a sound. After a few moments, he tried to focus through the mini-forest of sheep legs to see if Lewis was still there, but it was difficult to make anything out. He looked up, but all he could see was the underside of the nearest sheep. Its pink sheep dick stared at him with its single cyclopsian eye—making him think again of Polyphemus—and pissed in his face.

Albert remained frozen, fear now mingled with horror. Once the sheep was finished evacuating its bladder, Albert wiped off his drenched face with his sleeve, trying desperately not to throw up. After he had more or less collected himself, he decided to risk another glance. He slowly peered over the sheep's back once again. Lewis was gone. He had moved to the other side of the flock. In fact, all the members of the gang were on the opposite side. They appeared to be preparing to search the barn. He would never have a better chance.

His heart in his throat, Albert took a deep breath . . . and bolted to his feet. He charged through the remaining sheep, scattering them on either side, as he made directly for Curtis. Luck was on his side. He had almost finished untying Curtis's reins when one of the outlaws spotted him.

"Clinch!"

Clinch and the other members of the gang whirled in Albert's direction. They immediately drew their guns and started for him, but Albert swung into the saddle and spurred Curtis into a gallop. The outlaws raced to their mounts and broke into pursuit.

Albert leaned in hard as he pushed the horse faster than he ever had in his life. "I never make you go fast, buddy," he pleaded. "Give it to me today!"

Comprehending, Curtis took his speed up a half notch. Albert could hear the pounding of outlaw hooves behind him as Clinch and his men gained ground. When the surrounding vegetation diminished and the chase reached the open prairie, Albert knew he was in for the long haul. There was nowhere to hide out here. Nothing to do but keep running until escape or death won the day.

And then the gunfire started. The shots were deafening, and out of the corner of his eye Albert could see little geysers of dust erupting from the sand as the bullets struck the ground, several of them just inches away from Curtis's hooves. "Curtis, you outrun these guys, and I'm gonna take you to a horse whorehouse. You'll get so much horse pussy. Just *please, go faster.*"

The gang was still gaining. One of the bullets punctured a hole in the canteen attached to Curtis's saddle. Water sprayed out behind Albert as he kicked hard at Curtis's sides. Albert had never ridden so fast and so hard, yet he knew it was not enough. And then something caught his eye off to the left. He turned and saw a puff of black smoke on the horizon.

It was his only hope. He veered hard left just as a bullet whizzed by his right ear. He exhorted Curtis again and again, knowing it was useless—the horse's legs were already pumping at top speed. Finally, Albert crested a small rise and saw the train tracks below. The freight train was traveling on a perpendicular course to his own. He would get only one shot at this, but if it worked . . .

He headed straight for it. A few more bullets whistled by him, and then one grazed him on the ankle. He realized it was almost the exact same spot that Charlie Blanche had shot him not so long ago.

The train raced onward, and he raced toward the train. At the final instant, Curtis uncorked a last reserve of speed, evidently bottled for just such an occasion. Horse and rider dashed at the tracks a mere half second before the train barreled past.

For the moment, Albert was safe.

Clinch and his gang were forced to wait for the train to pass completely before they could resume their pursuit. The outlaw horses idled aggressively back and forth, fueled by the fury of their masters. At last, when the caboose whizzed by and shrank into the distance . . . Albert was gone.

Clinch stared darkly at the receding train as Ben galloped up beside him. "What the hell do we do now, Clinch?"

"Now," Clinch said, "we find my wife."

By the time dusk fell, Albert had managed to find a suitable spot to make camp. Not that he had any supplies—the well-stocked bag he'd prepared was still sitting on the floor back in his abandoned cabin. A small amount of water had remained inside the punctured canteen, but Albert had drained it hours ago. He would have to find water soon, or he'd be in real trouble. He might be a little hungry, but he could at least rest for the night and figure out his next move in the morning. And there was even a bit of green vegetation in the area, so Curtis wouldn't have to go to sleep on an empty stomach. God knew the horse deserved a good meal after the way he'd come through for both of them.

Albert hadn't realized he'd had it in him, but when he'd seen an open boxcar coming along the track, he'd known it was the difference between life and death. He'd gone at a hard gallop straight toward the side of the speeding train. Curtis had leapt into the open boxcar, and he and Albert had been carried off to safety. Albert had never loved the animal more than he did right now.

"Curtis, you saved both our lives today. As soon as we're out of this, I'm gonna find you some horse whores, just like I promised."

Curtis snorted his enthusiasm for the concept.

Albert ruffled the horse's mane affectionately. "Now," he said, turning his attention to matters of immediate concern, "how the fuck do you make a fire?"

THWACK!!

He was unconscious before he realized he was not alone.

Edward sat on the bed in his room above the shoe-repair shop, dressed only in his drawers. Ruth stood before him with a giddy smile on her face. She wore nothing but a simple chemise. It was a big night for both of them, and the special moment was now at hand.

"Okay, here we go." Edward grinned, his bare feet tapping the floor with nervous energy.

"Are you excited?" said Ruth.

"I am. I'm really pumped."

"Me too."

"This is gonna be my first vagina," he admitted with a blush.

"You've never seen one?"

"No. I feel like I should have a piece of cake or something. Y'know, to celebrate."

"Yeah, I'm actually a little nervous myself."

Edward giggled. "*You're* nervous? Wow, and you're a prostitute!"

"I know, right?" she said, joining in the laughter. "Okay. Ready?"

"Yup!"

Ruth pulled up her hem, exposing her womanhood.

Edward's bright, eager smile became flaccid, then finally disappeared. He stared in silence for a long while.

"What?" she finally asked with a furrowed brow.

"Um . . ."

"What's wrong?"

He pointed. "It's . . . *that* right there, right?"

"Yeah." She indicated. "It's from here to here."

"Huh." He put his chin in his hand ponderously and leaned back a bit with the air of a math professor piecing together a difficult equation. "It's . . . I . . . wow, I don't . . . I don't get it."

"You don't like it?"

"No, I—it's just—weird. It's a weird thing. It's like . . . someone wrapped a firecracker in roast beef."

"Well, yeah, but there's a lot more to it." She opened it up, showing him the rest.

His eyes snapped open in shock. "Oh! Oh, dear! Oh, my Jesus, Mary, and Joseph! Were you injured? Are you in pain right now?"

"No, Eddie, it's *supposed* to be like this."

"It is?" he asked in disbelief.

"Yeah. Well, I mean, maybe not *exactly* like this, but listen—it'll feel good. For both of us."

Edward calmed a bit. "Gosh, I'm sorta glad I didn't have that piece of cake."

She smiled comfortingly. "Eddie . . . just trust me."

Ruth extinguished the light, discarded the chemise, and climbed into bed with him. She eased his head gently back down onto the pillow and climbed on top of him, guiding his twitching penis inside her.

"Oh, boy," he said with alarm. "Okay, easy, now, I'm—*okay. Oh. Okay.* Okay, I see. Yeah, now I get it. 'Cause of the warm and the soft and—yeah. *Yes,* okay, yeah, God would want this."

The first moment of carnal pleasure Edward Phelps had ever experienced was almost immediately cut short when his amateur pounding was interrupted by an even harder pounding on the door.

Ruth sighed loudly with annoyance and climbed off him. She hastily threw on her chemise and padded across the room. When she opened the door, she found the last person she'd expected to see.

"Anna?"

"Ruth, can I come in?" Anna said, in a clear state of distress.

"Um, yes. Yes, of course."

Anna hurried into the room as Ruth shut the door behind her.

Edward sat up, scrambling to cover his nakedness with the sheets. "Don't come over here! I don't want you to see my penis."

Edward's penis appeared to be the last thing on Anna's mind. She had ridden straight out to the ridge from Albert's cabin, then realized she could not go any farther. Since she had been old enough to understand what her life really was, she had been running away from herself. She had denied the woman she wanted to be for too long, and it was time for that denial to end, at any cost—even death.

She knew her redemption lay with Albert. Unfortunately they'd been separated, and she did not know where he'd gone. She didn't even know if he'd escaped. So she'd backtracked to the cabin, which she found deserted. For lack of an immediate plan, she sought out Edward and Ruth back in town, but when she'd arrived at the saloon at dusk, the word was that Clinch and his men were out to hunt her down. And now here she was.

Anna ran to the window and looked out. From the upper level that housed Edward's apartment, she had a clear view of most of the thoroughfare. Almost immediately, she spotted them. Five figures, moving up the street, methodically entering each building. As they moved a little closer, she could make out their faces. It was Clinch, all right. As she watched them, trying to get a sense of their search pattern so she could strategize her escape route, he looked directly up at the window. Anna quickly closed the curtains. "Shit!" Had he seen her? She thought he'd made eye contact, but she couldn't be sure. "Ruth, I need a place to hide!" she said breathlessly. There wasn't much furniture in the room and no closet to speak of. Under the bed? Behind the dresser? Neither were promising choices. As they frantically looked for an option, they heard the sound.

Thump. Thump. Thump.

Ruth ran to the side window and looked out. "Oh, my God," she whispered. "The side stairs. He's coming up the side stairs!" The glass was warped and caked with dust, but there was no mistaking the shadowy figure making his ascent toward the apartment.

Anna ran to the window that faced the thoroughfare and pushed it open. She climbed out onto the roof, made her way carefully down the wooden planking, and jumped.

When she landed, she was face-to-face with Clinch.

At that same moment, the shadowy figure reached the top of the stairs and kicked open the apartment door. Ruth and Edward found themselves staring down the barrel of Lewis's pistol, his ratlike face scowling at them with accusation.

Edward extended his hands in an appeal for mercy. "Please don't shoot us on sex night!"

Lewis grunted angrily but left them in one piece.

"I'm not suggesting we run with this," said Edward when he and Ruth were alone, "but when he pointed that gun at us, my erection came back."

Albert blinked groggily as he regained consciousness. The world was dark and blurry. Everything was swimming in marsh water. He tried to lift his hand to rub his eyes but found that he was unable to do so. In addition, there was an intense pain in the back of his head. He was lying on his back on some sort of hard, narrow surface. It was terribly uncomfortable. When he looked up, he could make out a series of undefined shapes surrounding him from above. *Faces?*

He tried to get up, but his hands were bound tightly behind him. And then he realized he wasn't lying on his back at all. He was standing . . . tied to a post of some sort. He blinked hard a few more times, and the world coalesced into clarity. The shapes he had seen were indeed faces. Thirty of them, to be exact. Old faces, young faces, puffy faces, gaunt faces—and all wore expressions of hostility.

Apaches.

Albert looked down at his feet, knowing all too well what he would find there. *Kindling. They're going to burn me. Out of the frying pan and into the fire. Literally.* Albert had escaped Clinch and his gang by a hairsbreadth, only to wind up cooked like a turkey by a tribe of renegade Apaches. For about the millionth time in his life, Albert had the thought that had become as familiar as a pair of old shoes: *God, I fucking hate the West.*

Three of the Apache warriors approached him, holding lit torches. Astonishingly, one of them looked familiar. He'd seen drawings of this man, and one time even a photograph. It was the infamous Apache chief Cochise, who had earned a reputation as a force to be reckoned with for his resistance to the expansion of white civilization throughout the territory. *Jesus, I'm the last guy you should be killing,* thought Albert. *I hate white civilization as much as you do.*

Cochise raised his torch and spoke in the Apache language, "White man, because your people are such huge assholes, I am going to light you on fire."

The three Apaches moved toward the pyre and prepared to light the kindling.

Albert spoke suddenly. "*Stop!*"

The warriors moved back, startled. Not because of the word he'd said but rather because he'd said it in perfect Apache.

Cochise ordered his men to stand down for the moment. They complied but kept their torches at the ready. He then addressed Albert, once again in his native tongue. "How is it that you, an asshole, have the power to speak our language?"

Albert answered with perfect diction. "I am a nerd asshole. Since the other white assholes do not like me, even though I am one of their own, I have always kept to myself. Therefore, I have read many books, know many languages, and am good at math."

Another Apache spoke up from the group. "Quick, what is 27 times 89?"

"2,403," said Albert.

Several of the warriors murmured among themselves, aware that the white man had answered correctly.

"Why are you out here?" asked Cochise.

"Please untie me, and I will tell you."

Cochise turned to the two torch-bearing warriors. "Well, he speaks our language, which means there's no reason not to trust him."

Albert breathed a sigh of relief as they lowered their torches and cut him loose.

Some time later, Albert found himself sitting around a campfire with Cochise and about nine or ten of the other Apache warriors. It was a scenario he never would have imagined in a billion years. Nonetheless, they were anxious to hear his story and to know how and why he had wound up all the way out here by himself. He told them everything.

" . . . And after I escaped on the train, I rode like the wind," he concluded, "and the next thing I remember is waking up in your camp. And now I have no idea what to do."

Cochise regarded Albert for what seemed like a very long time, then turned and whispered something to the leathery-skinned Apache elder seated at his right. The elder slowly nodded. Cochise turned back to Albert. "I will show you the way," he said.

He gave a wordless hand signal to one of the younger warriors. The man rose from the circle and stepped away into the darkness. He returned a few moments later with a cactus bowl containing some sort of viscous liquid. The warrior handed the bowl to Cochise, who took a sip and then passed it over to Albert.

"What is it?" Albert asked uneasily.

Cochise gave him a meaningful stare. "Your path."

Albert didn't recognize the fluid in the bowl, but he had a pretty good sense of what it was, having just been through this with Anna and her goddamn cookie. "I'll freak out, I know it," he said, giving Cochise a look of severe apprehension.

"You won't freak out, I swear."

"You don't know me. I'm serious, I'm very sensitive to drugs."

"Nerd."

The other tribesmen joined in the taunting. "Nerd! Dork! Tool!"

Albert reluctantly submitted to the peer pressure. "Okay, fine!" He downed the rest of the liquid.

Almost instantly, the Apaches' taunting expressions shifted to shock and alarm. *"He drank the whole bowl!"*

Albert froze in panic. "What?"

"You drank the whole bowl!"

"Oh, shit! Oh, shit, is that bad?"

"That was for the entire tribe!" said Cochise. "You're totally gonna freak out and probably die. Good luck."

Albert's jaw hung open in terror as the world around him dissolved into a distorted hellscape. . . .

He tried to move his arms, but they remained locked at his side. Something was holding him in place. He looked down to see that his entire body was sandwiched between two brown, rough-looking sides of the same giant vise. Wait, not a vise . . . a walnut? Yes, a walnut. He was trapped in the center of an oversized walnut. But where the hell was he?

When he looked up, he saw stars. Countless stars. Never had he seen so many. But what terrified him was what he saw when he looked down: More stars. Thousands. He was floating above the sky, in the heavens, and there was no up or down. He could see, on all sides of him, other walnuts of various sizes circling the sun.

Somewhere off to his left, another light source flared up. Albert turned and was astounded to see a massive cloud of gas and dust expanding from a single point too far away to ascertain. Every color in the known spectrum was engaged in a sort of misty water ballet; there were even a few new colors

Albert had never seen before. New colors? *How was that possible? But before he could contemplate it further, the gas cloud contracted as quickly as it had expanded. The gorgeous multihued formation was drawn into a rapidly widening vacuum. A gaping hole opened up, like some horrific maw leading back to a dark time before creation that no living man should ever see.*

And then everything was sucked inside. The walnuts, the stars, the gas and dust, and Albert. The intensity of the pull flung him free of the nut in which he'd been confined, and he found himself being hurled at blinding speed through a vast tunnel, which that seemed to twist and turn at random like an agitated earthworm being poked with a twig by a sadistic child.

And then all at once he was on solid ground. He hadn't felt the impact, but nonetheless he was here, lying prostrate on an uneven surface. He lifted his head and spat out a mouthful of sand. He was back in the desert.

But as he struggled to stand, he saw that it was not his desert. Not the Southwest. There was no vegetation here, no rocks, no dirt—just sand. Miles and miles of sand, with dunes stretching all the way to the horizon. It looked more like the North African deserts he'd read about in books.

He was not alone. Something was here with him.

A dark shape momentarily blocked out the sun, and Albert heard a piercing SHRIEEEEK. He looked up just in time to see a massive black condor descending toward him from the sky. It was moving as fast as a locomotive and appeared to be nearly half the size of one as well. But that wasn't the only thing wrong with it. Its eyes glowed bright green, and it had fangs. *No bird that Albert had ever seen or heard of had fangs. This was a hellish demon-bird that looked as though it had burst into reality from a mythical tale created by some long-dead and best-forgotten savage civilization.*

Albert tried to scream, but nothing came out. So he ran. He ran as fast as he could, which in this nightmare world still felt like moving through molasses. Just as the condor was upon him, he lunged over the crest of one of the dunes, tumbled violently down a steep embankment—

—and crashed through a layer of solid ice.

Albert plunged deep into the frigid water beneath. He immediately swam for the surface but could find no opening. Beneath the solid ice, he was trapped. He began to panic again as he pounded on the frozen ceiling with both fists, his lungs aching with pressure as their final reserves of oxygen were depleted.

Then at last, just as the grip of unconsciousness tightened around his body, he found the opening through which he had fallen. With all his remaining strength, he pulled himself up out of the water, finding purchase on the snowy shoreline that rimmed the freezing pool. He stood up, dripping and shivering, and surveyed his surroundings. He was in an Arctic wilderness, and there was a blizzard in full force. Stinging snowflakes bit and snapped at his face at the same time that he became aware this was no ordinary tundra. There were tall palm trees peppering the landscape, so curiously equidistant from one another that they looked almost artificially placed. Each frond was a different color, which gave them a striking rainbow effect. But what drew Albert's attention more than anything else was the cabin. It was his cabin. Just plopped out here in the middle of this insane, otherworldly panorama. He ran toward it, partly out of curiosity and partly out of fear of death from pneumonia or hypothermia. He reached the cabin door and hurried inside.

It was his house, but empty. No—not completely empty. There was a lone rocking chair next to the cold, unlit fireplace. Because he had nowhere else to go, Albert walked to the chair and sat down.

Almost instantly the walls around him began to ripple. At first, he braced himself for another transition—Jesus, what's next, the moon?—but it was merely the room itself that was changing. The rippling intensified, turning the walls and floor into liquefied, ocean-like waves of wood and sod. And then, abruptly, it stopped.

The room was no longer empty. There were chairs, tables, paintings, and photographs on the walls. It was still Albert's cabin, but its personality had been entirely altered. It had been transformed into a cozy, beautifully decorated home. He almost didn't recognize it.

And there was Anna.

She was seated in a second rocking chair on the other side of the fireplace, which now roared and crackled and gave off a warm, comforting glow. Anna smiled wordlessly at Albert as she stitched some ornately embroidered words into a pillow: Don't go snackin' if you been tobaccin'. After a moment, she set down her stitchery and pointed off to his right.

When he turned, he noticed a small table that hadn't been there a second ago. On it sat a steaming cup of coffee. Albert felt himself smile. Although his clothes and skin were now somehow dry, he still felt an inner chill from the ice and snow. He could certainly use a cup of coffee. He picked it up and prepared to take a sip, but stopped as he looked into the cup. The coffee was spinning like a whirlpool. It was almost hypnotic, and soon he found that he could not take his eyes off it. He could still feel his *body placed firmly in the chair, but at the same time he had the distinct sensation that he was being pulled down, down, down into the eye of the whirl-pool.*

And then he was no longer inside the cabin but rather was sitting on a hard, ribbed surface. He looked down. Wicker. Wicker on the floor, wicker on the walls . . . no, not walls. I'm in a basket. *He scrambled to his feet, and his breath caught in his throat as he took in his latest surroundings.*

He was floating in a hot-air balloon surrounded by trees. But these trees were impossibly, fantastically tall. Whether Albert looked up or down, he could not see where they began or ended. The trunks simply receded to infinitesimally small points in the distance.

He felt the balloon quiver slightly. When he gazed up, he saw that the fabric above him now bore a gigantic face. A face he knew all too well. Foy's face. "Balloon moustache, balloon moustache," *it sang in echoey, dissonant, reverberating tones. Albert grimaced in repulsed confusion, but before he could react further, a dark shadow passed overhead. The black condor swooped down from above, ripping Foy's face to shreds with its massive talons. Unfortunately, the balloon itself was also in tatters, and Albert began to plummet fast. He let out a scream as he looked down and saw the trunks racing past him at blurring speed. Still, the ground had yet to make an appearance. His fall accelerated, and Albert could feel his face rippling from the force of the descent. His insides pushed angrily at the back of his throat like an invading army with a battering ram at the gate. Then, suddenly, with a hard, skull-rattling jolt, it stopped.*

He glanced up and found that the balloon had caught on a branch. He was swaying back and forth pendulously, and the branch looked ill-equipped to hold his weight for long. He looked down again and saw the forest floor at last.

It was a sea of raging fire.

The branch snapped.

Albert braced himself for death as the basket plummeted again and the flames rushed up to meet him—

THUD!

He landed on a patch of soft green grass. The impact had been harder than the others, and he thought for a moment that his nose was broken, or at least bleeding. But when he poked at it gingerly with his index finger, it felt intact. He struggled to his feet and looked around. He was standing in a wide-open field, surrounded at its perimeter by a thick layer of pine trees. It was an oddly silent place, bereft even of birdsong. And then he began to hear the clip-clop *of hooves. He turned toward the sound. Approach-*

ing from the distance was the most ornate horse-drawn carriage he had ever seen. It was a bright shade of purple, and was pulled by two milk-white mares bedecked entirely in gold-colored tack. The carriage came to a stop directly in front of Albert. The horses did not stir, but Albert got the distinct sense that they were waiting for him to act. He cautiously moved toward the side door and grasped the handle. When he opened it, his head spun.

Beyond the door was the interior of a Gothic church. It was dazzling in design, lusciously opulent in décor—and full. There had to be five hundred people in attendance, all lavishly dressed and all staring expectantly at Albert. Most were strangers, but some folk he recognized from Old Stump: Edward, Ruth, Millie, Doc Harper, Sheriff Arness—and Anna.

She was dressed in a flowing white wedding gown and stood at the altar, attended by Pastor Wilson. Her gaze was warm and welcoming as she beckoned him to approach. The magnetism of the vision was irresistible. Albert stepped through the doorway . . .

. . . and tumbled out the other side of the carriage. He felt the wind knocked out of him as his rib cage absorbed the impact. He pulled himself up, clutched his side in pain, and turned back toward the open door. The church was gone. All that remained was the inside of the carriage, which looked just like any other. Even the bright purple efferves-

cence of the surface had become dulled. He reached an arm inside, searching, grasping for any trace of the vanished mirage, but found nothing. Instead of disappointment, however, he felt something else. Anger. Something had tantalized him with this gateway to the life he wanted and then deliberately denied him access. It was then that Albert realized, with a wave of release, how tired he was of being a perpetual punching bag for the endless blows the western frontier hurled at him.

He heard the unmistakable shriek *of the condor. He looked up as the monstrous creature bore down on him from the sky once again, its eyes glowing an unearthly green, its white fangs glinting bestially in the sunlight. But this time, Albert did not run. Something tugged at his waist, and when he looked down he saw that he was wearing his gun belt. Without a moment's pause, he drew the pistol and fired several rounds at his avian attacker. To his frustration, the bullets did not pierce the bird's skin, instead bouncing off harmlessly. However, the bird did veer away from its trajectory and circled back up into the air. It swung around for another assault, and Albert fired at it again. His gut wrenched as he heard the* click-click *of an empty chamber. No more bullets.*

The condor dove directly for him. He was about to run when he noticed a bulbous feathered convexity between the condor's legs. A ball sack, *he real-*

ized. Completely exposed and unprotected. Could it be that easy . . . ? The bird came at him, shrieking with open jaws. As it overtook him, Albert kicked the ball sack as hard as he could with the toe of his boot. The condor let out an earsplitting, hellish scream that echoed all across the field as it spun away, head over tail, off into the sky, until it vanished to a pinprick of darkness against the sun.

Albert sat up with a violent start. The light was suddenly gone. He could feel a thick coat of perspiration descending the surface of his face. As he took in his surroundings, he realized he was still sitting around the campfire, with the Apaches watching him intently. The first pink ribbons of dawn were visible on the edge of the horizon. Albert felt a gentle hand on his shoulder. It was Cochise.

"Did you shoot the black condor and kick it in the balls?" asked the wizened old warrior.

Albert was startled. "Yes. How do you know that?"

Cochise's eyes crinkled as he gave Albert a warm, knowing smile. "It means that true courage does indeed lie within you. If you can trust in its power, then you may yet find happiness."

———

Several hours later, Albert stood facing the entire Apache tribe at the edge of their camp. He regarded Cochise with a look of gratitude. Albert had begun his odyssey as their prisoner, and now he was closing it out as the beneficiary of their wisdom and kindness.

"Thank you for everything, Chief Cochise. I don't know what I would've done without you."

Cochise gave him a look that was almost paternal. "There is an ancient proverb among my people: Sometimes the only way for a man to discover his true path is to take drugs in a group."

Albert nodded. "Thank you for letting me take drugs with you. I know what I have to do now."

He gave Cochise a long embrace, mounted Curtis, and waved goodbye. The Apaches watched as he galloped off toward his destiny.

The main thoroughfare of Old Stump was overcast and deserted as Clinch Leatherwood dragged his wife out into the center of the street, his pistol pressed against her side. Lewis, Ben, and the rest of the gang watched with amusement as their leader began his deadly theatrical display.

"All right, sweetheart," he whispered into her ear, his foul breath assailing her nostrils, "now we're gonna find out whether your little boyfriend gives a fuck about you." Clinch took out the gold pocket watch for which he'd shot a man not three months before. "He's got six minutes till noon. If he doesn't show, he's gonna be picking up pieces of you all over the street." Clinch shouted at the empty horizon. *"STARK!!"*

There was no answer. Anna stood stone-faced, ever the picture of courage. She knew she was going to die today, but she also knew she'd be goddamned if she'd give her bastard of a husband the pleasure of seeing her break. In reality, the last thing she wanted was for Albert to make an appearance. There was no way he stood a chance against Clinch. She already felt the regretful sting of her own betrayal, and she did not want to be responsible, indirectly or not, for his death.

For a moment, they all struck a morbid tableau: a large and sinister man with a reptilian gaze standing rigidly in the center of the street, a loaded pistol against his wife's ribs, his gang watching as if they were witnessing a carnival show rather than a prelude to murder, and dozens of goatish frontier faces with fearful eyes peering helplessly from windows, doorways, alleys, all too terrified to emerge. Even the sheriff watched from the safety of his office, displaying his usual ineffectiveness.

And then, from the distance, the sound of hooves. As they grew closer, Anna's heart sank even deeper. *No, Albert, no! Get out of here or he'll kill you too!*

Albert appeared astride his horse at the end of the thoroughfare. When he came to a halt, his clumsy, nerdish dismount only amplified her distress. Was he insane? He was a sheep farmer with one week of shooting practice under his belt, and he was going to go up against the deadliest outlaw in the West?

"Let her go, Clinch." To his credit, Albert's voice was steady.

Clinch gave Anna a loveless squeeze. "Well, now," he said with an evil grin, "true love conquers all, doesn't it, sweetheart?"

"Albert, don't be stupid!" she shouted desperately. "Get the hell out of here!"

Clinch twisted her arm, hard. "Too late for that," said the outlaw. "He's already been *real* stupid, haven't you, Stark? You've been with my wife."

Albert seemed to carefully measure his response. "Well, I mean, we haven't *done* it, if that makes a difference."

Clinch shoved Anna roughly toward Lewis, who restrained her firmly—and with far too much pleasure—and leveled his gun at the space between Albert's eyes. Albert stiffened, but held the other man's gaze. "Y'know, I hear you're a pretty tough guy, Clinch. Well, why don't you prove it? You and me. Gunfight. Right here, right now."

Clinch brightened visibly. He looked almost entertained, as if someone told him he was about to be treated to a puppet show. "You really do have a death wish, don't you?" he said with a grisly little cackle.

"*But*—" Albert raised a hand. "But let's make it interesting. One bullet apiece. One for you, one for me."

For a moment, Clinch actually looked caught off guard. "What?"

"Yeah. Empty all your bullets but one. Unless you think you need more than one to kill me."

Clinch hesitated. He certainly had no fear at all of this lowly, pathetic sheep farmer, but he also was clearly unable to calculate what Albert's angle was. He eventually seemed to decide it made no difference. His dark smile returned as he emptied the chamber of his pistol save for one round.

Albert did the same.

"Okay. On the count of three, we shoot," said Albert, a few beads of perspiration popping out on his forehead.

Clinch nodded.

Albert took a deep breath. "One . . . two . . ."

Albert fired.

He hit Clinch in the left arm.

Clinch looked down at the wound, then slowly lifted his gaze back to Albert, that awful smile spreading across his face in tandem with the blood. He let out a big guffaw that echoed eerily across the expanse of the empty town. "I been playing cards a long time, and I've never seen such a bad gamble, Stark. Where'd you learn to shoot?"

"Your wife."

"Aw, snap," whispered Edward from his doorway.

Clinch stopped laughing. He raised his gun and cocked it.

Albert dropped his own gun and raised both hands plaintively. "Look, before you shoot me . . . grant me a few last words. Please?"

Clinch sneered. "Why not? Yes, let's savor this moment."

"Okay, good. Thank you. Look—just promise me one thing. Let Anna live. Please. She didn't kiss me, I kissed her. So it's my fault." Albert paused in momentary thought. "I mean, she didn't tell me she was married, so it's kinda her fault too, I guess, so . . . yeah, actually, that's true. So maybe just shoot her in the leg? That seems fair, right?"

Anna gave him a *what-the-fuck* stare.

Albert went on. "And one more thing: My grandparents were Arabic, so if you'll indulge my religious beliefs here . . . Immediately before death, I'm

207

required by Muslim tradition to recite the Islamic death chant. This'll only take a moment." And Albert began to warble a stream of vocal dissonance that sounded like a goat being castrated.

Has he lost his fucking mind? Anna thought. It wasn't until he'd been at it for several seconds that she became aware of a change in Clinch. He was blinking rapidly. And he'd broken out into a sweat. He glanced around unsteadily, appearing to falter a bit. His aim drifted, until eventually his gun fell from his quivering hand. He seemed to be having enormous difficulty maintaining his balance.

"What the . . . what the hell is happening?" he grunted weakly.

Anna had the same question. *Is this witchcraft or something?*

Albert ceased his warbling and addressed Clinch again. "You know, Clinch, there are a million ways to die in the West. There's disease, famine, exposure, gunfights . . . and wild animals. You know, like snakes. And the interesting thing about snakes is, you don't even have to get bitten. All you have to do is get the venom into your system, and you're pretty much screwed. Let me tell you about a little trick some Apache friends of mine taught me recently: You take a certain amount of venom from a diamondback rattler and drain it into a hollowed-out bullet tip, and, you know what? You really only need one shot. Now, I knew my aim wasn't good enough to hit you anywhere important, but if I caught you by surprise . . . Well, Anna taught me enough to get me in the ballpark. And it didn't matter where I hit you, as long as the bullet broke the flesh. Because just a little bit of venom in an open wound is enough to kill a man if he's—"

"Albert. He's dead."

"Huh?"

It was Ruth who had spoken. She stood over Clinch's collapsed body. "He's dead. You killed him."

"Oh." It was true. Clinch lay unmoving on the ground.

"Did he hear all the smart stuff that I did?"

"No, I don't think so."

"Oh. Okay. It's still good, though."

A wide grin broke out across Anna's face as she elbowed Lewis in the gut. He doubled over in pain and surprise, just as the sheriff and deputy emerged from their office, guns trained on Clinch's men.

Anna ran to Albert and threw her arms around him, raining kisses upon him with all the passion of a parched castaway suddenly being given water. His lips melted into hers for a full minute before she pulled away, gazing at him with love, pride, and profound relief.

"Not bad, sheepboy," she said. "Not bad at all."

"Sorry I killed your husband." He felt at least some obligation to say it.

Anna took his hands in hers. "Albert . . . it's the sweetest thing anyone's ever done for me."

"Which is kinda fucked up, huh?"

"Yeah, it is kinda fucked up, isn't it?"

They kissed again. When they parted this time, Albert became aware that he was being observed. He turned to look behind him.

Standing there was Louise.

"Hey, Albert," she said flirtatiously.

"Oh. Hey, Louise."

"Listen, um . . . if you wanna . . . talk about things, I'd like that. I could come by your place later on tonight."

A very short time ago, Albert would have shot himself in the knee just to hear her speak those words. And now he felt nothing. It was not until that moment that he knew he was truly free. Free from her emotional grasp. Free to pursue happiness with someone who was ready to love him for the rest of his life.

"I can't, Louise." He smiled. "I really need to work on myself. But thank you for your interest."

He didn't see her face fall, as he was already walking away, hand in hand with Anna.

Anna turned to him with electrified eyes as something new occurred to her. "Y'know . . . you shot

Clinch Leatherwood. The deadliest gunman on the frontier. There's probably gonna be reward money."

"Huh. I didn't think about that."

"So, what are you gonna do?"

And that was how, in the warm Arizona summer of 1882, Albert and Anna Stark, newly wed in the little town of Old Stump, came to embrace beside his small cabin, in the center of a great flock of sheep five thousand strong. And through the gift of a new, mint-bright outlook fueled by a woman's love, Albert Stark found that he was happy to live in the West.